T0326267

Cambridge Farm Institute Series

General Editors:
T. B. Wood, M.A.
Sir E. J. Russell, D.Sc.

FARM ACCOUNTS

FARM ACCOUNTS

BY

C. S. ORWIN, M.A.

DIRECTOR OF THE INSTITUTE FOR RESEARCH IN AGRICULTURAL
ECONOMICS IN THE UNIVERSITY OF OXFORD

SECOND EDITION REVISED

CAMBRIDGE
AT THE UNIVERSITY PRESS
1924

CAMBRIDGE
UNIVERSITY PRESS

University Printing House, Cambridge CB2 8BS, United Kingdom

Cambridge University Press is part of the University of Cambridge.

It furthers the University's mission by disseminating knowledge in the pursuit of education, learning and research at the highest international levels of excellence.

www.cambridge.org
Information on this title: www.cambridge.org/9781316606926

© Cambridge University Press 1924

First published 1924
First paperback edition 2016

A catalogue record for this publication is available from the British Library

ISBN 978-1-316-60692-6 Paperback

NOTE

THIS edition of *Farm Accounts* has been completely revised and very largely re-written. A new example, based on the accounts of a Gloucestershire farm, has been substituted for the one used in the former edition, so as to bring the costs and values into accord with the changes that have taken place, and some new record-forms are introduced. An important omission has been made in the exclusion of Interest on Capital as an item of cost, but it is satisfactory to note that with this exception the additional experience of a further ten years has not indicated the need for a modification of any of the principles or methods advocated.

The author desires to acknowledge the assistance rendered by his colleague, S. J. Upfold, in this revision.

OXFORD, *July* 1924.

CONTENTS

*Broad Acre Farm labour analysis for week ended 11th May 1923 is available for download from www.cambridge.org/9781316606926

CHAPTER I

INTRODUCTORY

THE keeping of accounts in some form is a part of every business in connection with which payments are made and received. Even if it be only a rough note with the date and such particulars of a transaction as make it possible to render a bill, or if it be only a loose receipt, a record is kept, for the embarrassment and loss which have been experienced where the slight amount of trouble involved in this work is not taken, have taught the advantage of attending to it. Few men with a sense of what is proper will incur the humiliation of having it proved that they do not know how their financial affairs stand, but among farmers the revelation of shortcoming in this respect is too common, and it is surprising to learn how many attempt to manage their business without the assistance of any records. Putting aside such cases, however, which, as they come to light in arbitrations or elsewhere, meet with general disapproval, and assuming that some system of book-keeping is in use, the question is now being asked whether, with the progress that has been made in other directions in farming, the time has not come for a considerable extension of account-keeping, and whether a task which is now performed with something of a grudge would not far more than repay the labour bestowed on it if it were taken up and carried through in a willing and generous manner, exactly on the principle that, while a horse is a troublesome animal to feed and attend, he does something more than compensate for all the trouble he causes in the services he renders.

The backwardness of farmers in book-keeping is pro-
verbial, and the reason is not far to seek. Farming is an
ancient industry, and it has made wonderful progress
without the help of book-keeping. In its beginnings
everywhere it was an entirely different business from
what it is to-day. Farmers were frequently a self-
sufficient people. They could satisfy most of their needs
and desires by commodities produced on their own farms.
They bought little and sold little, and their wage-bills,
where there were wages, were settled largely in kind.
Book-keeping was then unnecessary, but whilst it is true
that we have travelled far from this state of affairs, the
progress has been step by step, and it is difficult in an
industry which develops so gradually to decide when
the time has arrived for a change in methods to meet
new conditions. It was different with the manufacturing
industries, which are of comparatively recent origin, and
which have depended on purchases and sales and on
cash-paid labour from the beginning, for, unlike farming
in its early stages, they carried book-keeping with them
as a necessary part of their equipment. But however
slowly it has come about, it is certain that a vast change
has taken place in the methods of agricultural production, and if we were to investigate the business carried
on by many farmers to-day, we should find in it a greater
resemblance to the most modern form of manufacture
than to the old time farming from which the business
has grown.

The keeping of financial records can be commended
on the ground that they add to the farmer's knowledge
something of the most practical and valuable kind.
Such records draw information and lessons out of the
farmer's own experience that are applicable to his own

business in a peculiar and exclusive manner, lessons that are otherwise unobtainable. The advantages of a good general education and of an agricultural education are now recognised, but we have not yet appreciated the benefit which a man derives from having his own experience, the organisation, management and practical working of his business, recorded in terms of profit and loss, and brought right back for him to work on in his next experiment. The education gained from well-directed account-keeping is not only more practical, but also it is more personal and intimate than any other kind of education. When a farmer's interest and energy are narrowed down to the serious business of making money, he produces some financial result, satisfactory or otherwise, which indicates his character as a farmer. Only accurate and sound financial records tell him what kind of man he is and what kind of man he ought to be in this respect. They show where losses were incurred owing to the pursuit of a line of farming the reasons for taking up which are still fresh in his mind, or over transactions into which he entered for reasons which he can recall. On the other hand, they show the methods of farming which have been most profitable. That is, they bring the results of his year's work before him when all the causes that contributed to produce them are also before him, and according to his skill in making use of them, a farmer may be guided into the soundest course of business. He may run a mixed farm and sell dairy produce, corn, bullocks, and sheep. One or more of these may always yield a much larger return than the others. One or more may usually show a loss. If this were brought out in records it would be possible to develop the more profitable lines, and to reduce (so far as the principles of mixed farming admit) the expenditure upon those less profitable. Similarly, in cases where there is only one form of produce with alternative methods of production, that method which leaves the largest profit would be shown, and could be adopted. Every farmer worthy of the name is an experimental farmer, and every year's work is an experiment, but what is the value of an experiment without an accurate record?

Granting this, it may nevertheless be remarked that there are already many text-books on the subject of Farm Book-keeping, but it is the merchant's system of book-keeping which has hitherto been applied to the farming industry, and by this it is impossible to attain to the objects already detailed. The merchant is concerned solely with the purchase and resale of goods, and his books must be framed to show at a glance the indebtedness of individuals to him or his indebtedness to them. But the farmer is a manufacturer, not a merchant; his transactions with individuals are few and do not, as a rule, need recording, whilst his profit or loss on his enterprise as a whole, can be obtained, with almost absolute accuracy, without any book-keeping at all. What he wants his books to tell him is the **cost of production** in the various departments of his farm, and his book-keeping must be arranged with this object alone. He must have a system which will enable him to determine the cost on the farm of everything turned out for sale. To do this he must also record the cost of all labour operations, mechanical, horse and manual, the cost of general establishment charges, and so forth. These details are of the greatest importance, for whereas in mixed farming it is often difficult to cut out an unprofitable branch, it is sometimes not even desirable so to do, for with all the details of the total cost before him, the farmer may be in a position to put his finger on the weak spot and to take steps to reorganise his methods so as to turn an unsuccessful into a successful line of production.

This argument is supported by the action first of Scottish farmers and more recently of those in England in the new enterprise of Milk Records, which are a complete precedent for the system of cost accounting under consideration. The various lines of farming and methods of production can be regarded for sake of example as so many milk cows, each containing possibilities of loss or gain. There were farmers not so long ago prepared to belittle and ignore the advantage of milk records. They would rely on good judgment, and on a good memory, and so forth. But most of the men who are keeping records to-day, had the experience of farming without their assistance. They had a generally correct idea about the merits of the different cows as milk producers, and they could tell whether a cow put on rather much flesh, or whether her milking period was rather short. But these same facts about the same cows placed before the farmers in the shape of cold figures have produced a revolution in many herds. The production of milk and the value of the herds have been enormously increased, proving once more that the most successful business management rests on figures which confirm or correct the judgment, and give confidence to the business man in deciding on his policy.

It is objected that the cost of production cannot be determined without the introduction of estimates into the calculation, and whilst this must freely be admitted there are no grounds for suggesting that these estimations of values are going to render useless the conclusions arrived at. An error of a penny or two in the cost of a quarter of corn, or of a hundredweight of beef, will not affect adversely the value of the determination to the farmer, and it will presently appear that the Cost system does, in fact, *diminish* the errors due to faulty estimations of value, for by it the actual cost of production is substituted in many places for them (see p. 21).

Another objection that has been raised against cost account-keeping is its difficulty. Transactions are carried through away from home and sometimes without bills; labour is employed at a distance from the house and the work is often changed. But it does seem unsatisfactory to spend money without keeping a record of its destination, and to allow things to slip, simply because it is difficult to grip them. This work of keeping records is being done on a number of farms in England and Scotland and on a much larger number in the United States and on the Continent. Like milking cows, like feeding all live-stock, it requires to be done every day, and this, which is one of its chief merits when the first difficulty is overcome, seems to be the greatest obstacle to its performance.

It has been stated that a properly designed system of accounts should have one aim and object only, namely that of enabling the farmer to ascertain the cost of producing the things sold off his farm, and the meaning of this must be fully appreciated. It is of the greatest importance to adhere strictly and exclusively to the method of getting at what it costs the farmer to produce whatever he sells, for this is the only information worth getting, and it gives everything that is required. The price when anything is sold can then be compared with its cost to the farmer, and the comparison enables him to tell at once how he stands with regard to profit or loss on any transaction.

The principle is simple. It is that when a farmer begins to produce anything, he traces the cost right through the process of production until he realises the value of the product by sale. It is no new principle; the application of it was advocated by Arthur Young and by subsequent writers in the first half of the nineteenth century. At the present day in America, and in most Continental countries, the organisation of the farm through the accounts is recognised as a definite and highly important study, and it has been neglected far too long in this country. The need is now admitted. It is felt that agricultural education can no longer proceed solely upon scientific and technical study, and that the application of technical skill and scientific knowledge must be controlled and tested by financial results. High quality stock, and magnificent crops may be the result not of efficiency but of waste and extravagance, and the good farmer is he who can utilise his land, capital and labour to produce the greatest monetary return, and not necessarily the most produce. It is only by accident that true efficiency of this kind is achieved without the accountancy test.

CHAPTER II

FARM VALUATIONS

In opening accounts, either for the first time, or at the beginning of a fresh period, the first matter for consideration is **capital**. Capital is the money invested in the farm, and the things over which it is spread (live stock, implements, tillages, etc.) are the farmer's assets. Nothing can be done until these assets have been valued. The method of valuation will depend upon whether the accounts are being started, or whether they are merely entering upon another year. In the first case, the valuation will be a matter of estimation. It is important to remember that this estimated valuation will only apply for one year because, in the second case, the records of the foregoing year will enable the farmer to assign real values, for the most part, to his assets, that is to say, the cost of their production.

Assuming the first case, the procedure in valuation is as follows. Beginning with the live stock, take a note-book and make a list of the **horses**, putting down the names and value of each, and the total value of the lot[1].

This Inventory-book will start thus:

INVENTORY and VALUATION of the Live and Dead Stock, Tenant-Right, etc. on Broad Acre Farm.

	1923	1924	1925	1926
Horses	£ *s.* *d.*			
Captain, br. g. . .	32 10 0			
Charlie, br. g. . .	12 0 0			
Grey mare . .	18 0 0			
3 year old colt . .	25 0 0			
2 year old colt . .	15 0 0			
Yearling filly . .	10 0 0			
(And 10 other horses	134 0 0)			
	£246 10 0			

[1] This example and all those that follow are taken, except where otherwise stated, from actual accounts kept by tenant-farmers in various parts of Britain.

By using a wide book, and leaving space at the bottom for future purchases, a period of several years may be covered, and the trouble of making successive yearly valuations much reduced.

Cattle must next be valued, and the breeding herd and the remainder of the cattle must then be grouped together in classes, such as "cows," "heifers in calf," "two year old bullocks," "yearlings," "calves," etc. and valued at so much per head:

	1923	1924	1925	1926
Cattle	£ *s.* *d.*			
46 cows in milk and in calf @ £25	1150 0 0			
Bulls				
1 2-year old . .	15 0 0			
1 yearling . .	12 0 0			
	£27 0 0			
Heifers				
2 in calf @ £20 .	40 0 0			
Calves				
3 @ £3 . . .	9 0 0			
3 @ 50s. . . .	7 10 0			
3 @ £2 . . .	6 0 0			
	£22 10 0			

Sheep and **pigs** are entered in the same way by grouping them in classes, and then valuing them at so much per head in each class.

Poultry too must be included, and the following is a specimen entry:

		1923			1924		1925	
	No.	Value			No.	Value	No.	Value
Poultry		£	*s.*	*d.*				
Pullets @ 4*s.*	115	23	0	0				
2 year old hens @ 3*s.*	159	23	17	0				
3 ,, @ 2*s.* 6*d.*	152	19	0	0				
Cockerels @ 10*s.*	5	2	10	0				
2 year old cocks @ 3*s.*	4		12	0				
Chickens @ 6*d.*	100	2	10	0				
		£71	9	0				

Before passing on to the Dead Stock an important point remains for discussion. It has been stated that the Live Stock must be inventoried and valued, but nothing has been said as to how the valuation is to be made. Certain classes of live stock are subject to sudden and extreme fluctuations in market value; for example, those who were farming in the year 1920 will recall the very heavy fall in the price of sheep during the following winter, and men who bought sheep at the spring, and even at the autumn, sales found themselves faced with an actual loss per head in the year following without taking any account of the cost of keep, etc. The same was true in the case of cattle. The same position may confront the breeder of pedigree stock for the Foreign Market, for an outbreak of Foot and Mouth Disease, like that in the year 1922, may suddenly reduce the value of such stock by fifty per cent., or even more. The question thus arises, what is the correct method by which to value breeding flocks and herds which, in the ordinary course of management, will not be realised? Are they to be valued at the market price of the day, however much it may be inflated or depressed from transient causes, or are they to be valued at some figure constant from year to year whatever the market may be? It is a controversial question, and the two alternatives may best be shown by an example. A man has a breeding flock which he keeps at a hundred head from year to year. He valued them in the autumn of 1919 at 90s. per head, being a little less than current market value. In the autumn of 1920 when he was making up his accounts for the past year, he found that his flock was worth some 140s. per head judged by the prices of the day, and he valued them accordingly. Thus his books showed him a profit (neglecting for the moment all other factors) of 55s. per head on his flock, or £275 in all. Now the value of all classes of sheep fell very severely in the latter part of 1921, and in the autumn the farmer reckoned up the markets and valued his ewes once more at 90s. Thus, during the second year they had apparently lost him 55s. per head, or £275 in all. He has had the same head of stock during the whole two-year period, he has not traded with it, and yet his books show a large profit during the first year and a serious loss during the second. Now this profit has never been in the bank, nor, indeed, could it have been realised in any shape or form, for it is assumed that the system on which the farm was run required that a hundred ewes should be maintained on it. For the same reason the apparent loss in the second year is not a real loss, and thus it is evident that this system of valuing breeding stock at market prices is apt to produce "paper" profits and "paper" losses.

Now, turning to the other alternative, by which breeding stock is valued at a constant figure year by year, the farmer in the example taken would probably have valued his ewe flock in 1919 at, say, 80s. per head, as being a figure below which the market price was never likely to fall, and he would have kept to this figure during the big prices in the early part of the year following, and also during the subsequent fall, so that his books would show neither "paper" profit nor "paper" loss. He puts a fixed value on his flock, a value which he is reasonably confident it would always realise, and he leaves it at that, regarding the flock as a factory for turning out mutton and wool, and his profit or his loss on his sheep-stock for the year depends on the cost of production and the market value of these commodities only. It must be understood that the system of valuing at a constant price applies not only to *breeding* flocks and herds where these are maintained at approximately the same number from year to year, and not offered for sale in the ordinary course of management, but also to the other classes of live-stock.

On the whole the writer recommends the "fixed value" system. An objection to this is that the farm books should show the exact realisable value of the farmer's assets at the date to which the accounts are made up, but where this value is liable to sudden and violent fluctuations before realisation is likely to be effected it seems very desirable to adopt some other standard.

As regards the valuation of the rest of the live stock, horses bred, or bought as yearlings, may safely be valued at £6 for each year's growth up to seven years, after which they should be depreciated by, say, £4 per annum until they stand in the books at £2. This method assumes an average maximum value of £42 per horse, and an average life of 18 years. Horses bought must, of course, be valued at cost, and each should be depreciated by such annual sum as will leave them in the books at about £2 per horse by the time they reach the age of 18 years[1].

Other classes of stock which have been bred or bought are best grouped in convenient classes, and valued in the same way, year by year, according to a constant scale of values.

Having now dealt with live stock, the valuation of the **dead stock** follows, and it includes, of course, such things as wagons and carts, implements of all sorts, machines, tools, utensils and so forth. A complete inventory of all these things must be made and a value assigned to each. It will save a great deal of trouble later on to group the implements, etc., under headings to correspond with the various departments of the farm, milk churns, cow-ties, for example, being placed under "cattle," and ploughs, harrows, manure-distributors, binders, etc., under "crops," whilst items which cannot thus be allocated, such as carts of all descriptions, are headed "general purposes."

All these things must be valued at the outset at market value, or if they are new, at cost, and in each succeeding year provision must be made for the depreciation which has occurred through use and age. The usual way of providing for depreciation is to knock off a fixed percentage at the close of the year, from the total value when the year began. This is objectionable because it is only a rough approximation, and because the percentage deducted is very often insufficient, particularly in the case of implements bought new. The better plan is to consider each implement by itself, and to assign it a life. The depreciation will then be got by

[1] The figures given apply to the ordinary type of good-class agricultural horse. Horses of any other class may be valued on the same principle, but from a different initial figure.

EXAMPLE OF

Implement	Cost (or Value)			Life	Annual Depreciation			Limit of Depreciation		
	£	s.	d.	Years	£	s.	d.	£	s.	d.
For Horse Labour:										
2 sets brass mounted harness	6	0	0	12		10	0		10	0
1 set silver do. . . .	3	3	0	9		7	0		10	0
4 sets cart harness . .	8	0	0	10		16	0	2	0	0
(And other items . . .										
For Cattle:										
4 18-gallon steel churns .	5	0	0	10		10	0		None	
Whitewashing machine .	2	0	0	8		5	0		None	
(And other items . . .										
For Crops:										
Manure distributor . .	10	0	0	10	1	0	0	2	0	0
3 1-way ploughs . . .	10	0	0	20		10	0	1	10	0
1 cultivator	5	0	0	20		5	0		5	0
(And other items . . .										
For Poultry:										
2 large lean-to pens . .	2	0	0	20		2	0		None	
10 black pens	5	0	0	10		10	0		None	
(And other items . . .										
For Dairy:										
Milk float	8	0	0	16		10	0	1	0	0
,, ...	14	0	0	20		14	0	1	0	0
Cooler for milk . . .	4	10	0	20		4	6		None	
(And other items . . .										
For General Use:										
Oil engine	30	0	0	5	6	0	0	10	0	0
Lorry	22	10	0	20	1	2	6	4	0	0
Cart	14	0	0	20		14	0	3	0	0
(And other items . . .										

IMPLEMENT VALUATION

Value in																	
1923			1924			1925			1926			1927			1928		
£	s.	d.	£	s.	d.	£	s.	d.	£	s.	d.	£	s.	d.	£	s.	d.
6	0	0	5	10	0												
3	3	0	2	16	0												
8	0	0	7	4	0												
24	5	10)	22	10	0												
£41	8	10	£38	0	0												
5	0	0	4	10	0												
2	0	0	1	15	0												
25	2	0)	23	0	0												
£32	2	0	£29	5	0												
10	0	0	9	0	0												
10	0	0	9	10	0												
5	0	0	4	15	0												
67	12	6)	64	5	0												
£92	12	6	£87	10	0												
2	0	0	1	18	0												
5	0	0	4	10	0												
23	18	0)	21	0	0												
£30	18	0	£27	8	0												
8	0	0	7	10	0												
14	0	0	13	6	0												
4	10	0	4	5	6												
159	4	2)	140	10	6												
£185	14	2	£165	12	0												
30	0	0	24	0	0												
22	10	0	21	7	6												
14	0	0	13	6	0												
118	15	9)	114	5	0												
£185	5	9	£172	18	6												

dividing the cost or value by the number of years' life. Many tools and implements will always have a certain value, whatever their age, if they are kept in repair, so that it is not always desirable to depreciate the value of an article down to nothing. A "limit of depreciation" is fixed, and when that figure has been reached, no further deduction is made, but the article is carried forward year by year at the same price. To take an example, a set of harrows may be worth 50s., and it will be safe to give them a life of ten years. This means that 5s. per annum must be deducted for depreciation, but if the harrows are kept in repair, they will always have a certain value, say 10s., so that after eight years, when the harrows will stand in the inventory at 10s., no further depreciation need be allowed.

This may appear for the moment a somewhat complicated and troublesome method of valuation, but by ruling the Inventory-book in the manner shown on the preceding page, the operation becomes a very clear and simple one, whilst it has the great advantage of reasonable accuracy. The value of each group of implements in any year and the depreciation on them become, first, a sum in subtraction and then a sum in addition. Several years can be provided for, but to avoid confusion in the future it must be remembered to leave a considerable space at the end of each group when writing out the inventory for the first time, to allow for purchases in the coming years.

Having dealt with these matters, the farmer must pass on to the valuation of **hay, straw,** and **corn.** On farms with a Lady-day entry none of these things will be very considerable, but in the case of Michaelmas entries they form important items. Measure the hay, and the straw and corn ricks, and find their contents in cubic yards by the ordinary rules of mensuration, and then allow 10–12 yards to the ton for hay, and about 26 yards to the ton for straw. When measuring, be careful to make ample allowances for outsides and tops, especially in the case of the hay. Having got the weights, the hay and straw are valued at so much per ton, taking either the *market* value or the *consuming* value according to the custom of the country, records of actual costs not being available.

In some districts it is usual to value the straw at per acre instead of at per ton, and this, of course, is the only possible way of valuing corn in stack. Make a note of the acreage which grew the unthreshed grain, and then estimate the crop, from your recollection of it, in quarters per acre. A value can then be assigned to it, from the quality of a rubbed-out sample, remembering to make an allowance of about 3*s.* 6*d.* per quarter for the cost of threshing and delivery. The specimen accounts which are being given as examples in this book relate to a farm with a Lady-day entry and there happens to be no hay, straw or corn in stack for valuation. Falling back on the imagination, the entry in the Inventory-book might be:

Grain.

The produce of 50 acres wheat in ricks, 250 quarters @ 40*s.*	£500. 0*s.* 0*d.*
The produce of 75 acres barley in ricks, 300 quarters @ 28*s.*	£420. 0*s.* 0*d.*

The inventory and valuation of threshed corn in the granary follows, and the whole is then totalled up.

Hay and Straw.

Stack meadow hay, about 17 tons	£45. 0*s.* 0*d.*
Stack barley straw, about 22 tons	£22. 0*s.* 0*d.*

The next matter for consideration includes all those things coming under the general heading of **tenant-right**, that is, cultivations, growing crops, unexhausted manures, etc. The farm is gone over field by field and all cultivations, seeds and manures since the last crop are recorded and valued. Cultivations are valued according to cost, at so much per acre, seed at cost and sowing, and manures at cost and spreading. On a Lady-day farm, there will be the wheat crop, the clover seeds, and possibly spring-corn, some catch crops and tillages for roots, together with labour and manures on grass-land, all to be valued. Taking the accounts of the farm already quoted by way of illustration, the entry in the Inventory-book will appear thus:

Nine Acre Field, 9 a. 2 r. 0 p. (Arable).

2¼ acres lucerne, 2nd year.   7¼ acres wheat after seeds.

		£	s.	d.	£	s.	d.
2¼ acres lucerne	@	3	0	0	6	15	0
7¼ acres—ploughed . . .	„		15	0	5	8	9
3 times harrowed .	„		2	0	2	3	6
21 bushels seed corn	„		5	0	5	5	0
drilled	„		5	0	1	16	3
10 loads dung[1] . .	„		5	0	18	2	6
					£39	11	0

Elm Field, 15 a. 0 r. 0 p. (Pasture).

		s.	d.	£	s.	d.
15 acres chain harrowed . .	@	2	0	1	10	0

and so on for the remaining fields.

On a Michaelmas farm there will be the fallows and fallow crops, the clover seeds, the tillages and manure for wheat and beans, and perhaps some catch-crops, and manures on grass. The valuation follows precisely on the lines of the Lady-day example.

[1] For valuation of dung see p. 34.

The principle to follow in the valuation of the items composing the Tenant-right calls for some consideration. In every district the local valuers have a fixed scale of allowances according to which payment is made to a tenant on quitting his holding, and whether it be the most equitable or not it is probably best to recognise it when starting accounts for the first time, because there are no records of the real costs to substitute for it.

Sometimes a farmer may be called upon to effect certain improvements on his holding of a more or less permanent nature. Under this heading may be included such things as liming, drainage, planting fruit, erecting buildings, and so forth. This is not the proper place in which to go into the details of the valuation of all such things, and it will be sufficient to say that the general principle to be followed in these matters is identical with that recommended for the valuation of implements (see p. 13). Decide upon the probable life of the improvement, and then write off the necessary depreciation each year from its initial value[1].

The only subject remaining for appraisement is the stocks of foods and manures which may be on hand at the end of the year. These are listed and valued at cost, including carriage.

Foods in Store.

		s. d.	£ s. d.
96 tons mangolds . . . . . @		14 0	67 4 0
Purchased feeding stuffs (give details)			45 15 6
			£112 19 6

[1] Sometimes the "life" is determined in quite another way. In a case known to the author a farmer having taken a 21 years' lease of a farm proceeded to build a pair of cottages on it. Their probable life would be 100 years or more, but for his purposes it had to be taken as 21 years.

Manures, etc. in Store.

		£	s.	d.	£	s.	d.
4 tons superphosphate	@	2	12	3	10	9	0
4 „ basic slag	„	2	12	0	10	8	0
4 „ kainit	„	2	19	0	11	16	0
5 tons 2 cwt. salt	„		15	9	4	0	4
Sawdust					20	0	0
					£56	13	4

Nothing further need be said here upon the subject of the valuation of the capital invested in the farm when starting accounts for the first time. There may be deductions from the total for dilapidations, that is, for tenant's repairs neglected, for foul land, for hedging and ditching to be done, etc., but these are subjects for special valuation and fortunately they are not incidents essential to every tenancy, and as they will not appear in the accounts of a properly managed farm they need not be discussed here.

Having thus completed the valuation, it will be convenient to summarise it in this way:

Summary of Valuation.

	£	s.	d.	£	s.	d.
Horses				246	10	0
Cattle—cows	1150	0	0			
bulls	27	0	0			
heifers	40	0	0			
calves	22	10	0			
				1239	10	0
Poultry				71	9	0
Cultivations, etc. (giving details of crops, or fields)				153	3	8
Stocks on hand—foods . . .	112	19	6			
manures . .	56	13	4			
				169	12	10
Implements—for horse labour .	41	8	10			
„ cattle . . .	32	2	0			
„ crops . . .	92	12	6			
„ poultry . .	30	18	0			
„ dairy . . .	185	14	2			
„ general use . .	185	5	9			
				568	1	3
				£2448	6	9

Such a valuation will serve when accounts are being started, but after the first year a different and a better system by which to value the capital in the farm must be adopted. The method of appraisement on a market value basis just detailed is at best an expedient, rendered necessary by the fact that data for more accurate calculations are not available, and the universal application of it year after year is unsound and leads to false conclusions. The proper course is to carry forward all uncompleted transactions from one year to the next *at their cost*. The approximate market value can be ascertained at any moment, and thus, by having the cost always before him in his books, the farmer is able to determine the most favourable time for realisation. Take the case of a bunch of calves raised on the farm; as yearlings their cost appears in the books, as two-year-olds again their cost is shown, and when they are sold fat off the farm the total cost is known and a comparison with the price realised is possible. Not only can this final comparison be made, but at any intermediate stage the knowledge of cost enables the farmer to decide whether it will be more profitable at current market prices to sell, say, his steers as stores at two years, or to finish them on the farm. Under the prevailing system of valuation at market price, the cost of the calves is lost sight of at the end of the first farm-year following their birth or purchase, by the substitution of their approximate market value, and thereafter the account is worthless to the farmer as a record of what he has done, and as a guide to his future actions.

The principle arises again in the valuation of home-grown foods fed to stock and the farmer or student must be perfectly clear upon it, for it is fundamental.

The fact that the market value principle has been advocated in this country for so long, and that it has been so positively re-asserted in recently published books[1], makes it necessary to deal with it at some length. In discussing the question Prof. Warren, of Cornell, gives an example which is itself the best possible refutation of the principle he advocates. He says: "No subject seems to be more generally misunderstood than the relation of crops to stock. The usual theory seems to be that if corn and hay can be easily and cheaply grown, they should be fed to live stock. Perhaps the basis of this error is the absurd practice of some institutions of charging feed to animals at the cost of producing it rather than what it can be sold for, less the cost of marketing. Some farmers are able to produce hay at a cost of £1 per ton. On other farms it costs £5. When this is charged to cows, it should be counted at its selling value. The cost has nothing to do with the value. The farmer who produced it at £1 might feed it to steers and get £1. 12s. 6d. for it; by this means he could make a profit on the two things, and steers might be hailed a very profitable enterprise. This sort of figuring misleads some farmers. If hay is worth £3 a ton on the market, a farmer is very foolish to sell it to steers for £1. 12s. 6d., no matter what it cost him."

Since the adoption of this practice, which Prof. Warren describes as absurd, is advocated by the present writer, it is necessary to justify it, and Prof. Warren's figures and illustrations provide the material for this. In one case hay costs £1 a ton to produce, in another it costs £5, and Prof. Warren, assuming the market price of hay to

[1] *Farm Management* by G. F. Warren, Professor of Farm Management in the Cornell University, New York, to mention one.

be £3, suggests that for record-keeping the cost should
be abandoned in both cases and the market price substituted. Clearly this sweeps away the principle of cost,
and information as to facts, as to what has happened,
is lost. A sum of £2 is added to the £1 which the hay
actually cost one of the farmers, whilst a sum of £2 is
deducted from the £5 which it actually cost the other,
and with this misrepresentation of their financial experience their accounts are carried on. If the first farmer
feeds 20 tons of hay to his bullocks, his accounts will
make him believe that they cost him £40 more than they
actually did, and if the second farmer feeds 30 tons of
hay, his accounts will show that they cost him £60 less
than was the fact. The principle will be the same in all
crops fed to stock, the farmers will no longer know how
they stand, and the error will increase with the magni-
tude of the enterprise.

The mistake is due to the departure from the method
of recording only what the farmer does. He never sells
his own hay to his own bullocks, and he will only confuse
himself if he goes through a process in his books which
does not correspond with anything in his practice.
Another cause of the mistake is the attempt to get a
comparison of profits at a wrong stage in the process
of production.

It is assumed that the farmer can tell what the hay
is worth to the bullocks. This seems to be impossible.
Accounts can show what bullocks cost, what hay, cake,
turnips and labour cost, but they cannot tell what
proportion of the bullocks' value is due to hay, and what
to turnips and cake, and it is not necessary that they
should. The time to compare the relative gains or
losses on the production of hay and bullocks is when

their cost of production is known, and both have been sold.

In the second and subsequent years, then, all such things as growing crops, hay, corn, straw, tillages, store and fatting stock, are valued by the simple process of carrying them forward in the accounts at cost price. Breeding stock and implements are, of course, valued upon the principles already stated (see p. 10 and p. 13).

CHAPTER III

FARM RECORDS

Manual and Horse Labour. Foods. Manures.

HAVING completed the valuation of the capital, the next step is to consider how the daily operations on the farm can best be recorded to enable proper account of them to be taken.

Manual labour suggests itself first of all and almost any form of labour-sheet which enables one to put down the daily occupation of each man employed on the place will serve. On the next page is an example which may be recommended.

This form is designed with a view to ascertaining the cost of labour. The name of the man comes first, and then follow columns in which can be recorded his work each day. Taking the year as a whole, it will be found that on most days each man is employed upon one job for the whole day, but owing to bad weather and other causes this is not invariably the case, and when a man is employed on various jobs his time must be divided. The division should always be done with care, and the American practice of dividing each man's time into

EXAMPLE OF FARM LABOUR-SHEET
BROAD ACRE FARM

TIME-SHEET OF J. SMITH FOR WEEK ENDED 11TH MAY, 1923

Sheet to be entered up every evening, and the exact time in hours
to be charged to each separate job.

Description of work and as far as possible amount done	Ordinary time	Weekday Overtime	Sunday Overtime	Piece Work £ s. d.	Horses used	No. of field, or job where employed
1st day:						
Attending horses .	2					Stables
Ploughing . . .	3				2	Field 17
Chain harrowing .	5				2	,, 6
2nd day:						
Attending horses .	1					Stables
Feeding pigs . .	1					
3rd day:						
Attending horses .	2					Stables
Carting farmyard manure . . .	8				1	To heap
4th day:						
Attending horses .	2					
Carting and applying liquid manure .	8				1	Field 10
5th day:						
Attending horses .	2					Stables
Mending fence .	5					Field 3
Carting and applying liquid manure .	3				1	,, 10
6th day:						
Attending horses .	2					Stables
Carting farmyard manure . . .	8				1	To heap
7th day:						
Attending horses .	2					
Carting feeding oats	5				2	From Station to Farm
Carting farmyard manure . . .	3				1	To heap
Total						

Summary of Wages and Piece Work:

		£	s.	d.
......60...Hours ordinary time @ 7d.		1	15	0
.... ,, weekday overtime @ . . .				
2 ,, Sunday overtime @ 9d.			1	6
Total Wages		1	16	6
Piece Work and extras		.	.	.
		£1	16	6

Deductions:

	£	s.	d.
Cottage Rent			
Milk, 7 pints @ 1½d.	10½		
Potatoes @............			
Insurance (Employee's Contrib.) . .	5	1	3½
Net Amount due to Worker	£1	15	2½

Employer's Initials...C. S. O. *Worker's Initials*...J. S.

hours[1] is to be recommended, especially where there is much broken time.

The spaces headed "Horses" which follow each day's work are for use in recording the horse-labour and will be dealt with later (see p. 27).

After the columns for time worked comes one for the field, or job, to facilitate the analysis.

The total time worked during the week is cast upon the foot of the sheet, and the proper wage due to the man can then be worked out, the extras added, and deductions made for rent, insurance, etc.

No mention has been made of piece-work but this can be recorded in a column on the same sheet. So far as the accuracy of the accounts is concerned, it is not necessary to work out the cost of piece-work *per day*, as the total cost can be charged to the proper department of the farm without difficulty. For the information of the farmer, however, the cost per day should always be worked out where possible, so that he can see how much his men are earning for the various jobs.

Any lump sums paid under certain local conditions of service, such as "Michaelmas-money," "lambing-money," and so forth, are taken direct to the "Labour Account" in the ledger, as will presently be described.

Having thus recorded the men's work, it must be analysed. The neatest plan is to use a book, or sheets, ruled with a series of columns as shown on the page adjoining. The columns are headed with the names of the various departments of the farm, and the work done and the horses used by each man during the week are entered in hours under the appropriate headings.

All the men are treated in a similar way, and then

---

[1] See labour-sheet on p. 442 in *Farm Management*, by G. F. Warren.

the various columns are totalled up at the foot of the page, so that the total hours of work and cost of piecework for each department of the farm during the week is shown, and also the work of horses engaged. These totals are carried forward week by week to the end of the year.

The wages paid each week, and the value of the allowances made to the men are entered in the "Labour Account" in the ledger (see p. 86). Thus, at the end of the year the farmer knows the total number of hours worked, and their total cost. A division sum will give him the cost of one hour's labour, and this, when multiplied by the number of hours worked in each department of the farm, will give the cost of the labour expended on each department.

Horse–labour next calls for attention, and this is a matter fairly easily dealt with. Whatever form of labour-sheet is used for the men must also provide the means for recording the number of horses working with them on any job. Referring to the labour-sheet, and the labour-analysis sheet first given, the method of entering the horses, analysing their work, and totalling up the number of days or hours worked in each department of the farm will be apparent at a glance. The way in which the cost of the horse-labour is ascertained from the number of days worked is dealt with later (see p. 135).

The recording of **foods consumed** ought to be a matter of the utmost simplicity, but as a matter of fact it frequently presents more difficulty than anything else. Every farmer should know how much cake, corn, hay, straw, roots, etc., is being fed to the various classes of stock on his farm, and no doubt the great majority of them do know. On the other hand, it is a very common experience to be told in answer to an enquiry as to the ration of, say, some cows—"Oh! I let them have all they can eat." More particularly does this apply to bulky foods such as hay and roots, but even where the men are given definite instructions they are frequently apt to observe them very indifferently or to vary them

Statement of Stock, and of Feeding-stuffs consumed.

Class of Stock	No. at beginning of week	No. born	No. bought	No. transferred in	Total	No. died	No. sold	Total died and sold	No. transferred out	No. at end of week
Horses . .	6	.	.	.	.	.	.	.	.	6
Colts . .	4	.	.	.	.	.	.	.	.	4
Nags . .	2	.	.	.	.	.	.	.	.	2
Pony . .	1	.	.	.	.	.	.	.	.	1
Dry cows .	13	.	.	.	.	.	.	.	2	11
Cows in milk	16	.	.	2	18	.	.	.	.	18
Yearlings .	12	.	.	.	.	.	.	.	.	12
Calves . .	43	2	.	.	45	.	.	.	.	45
Bull . .	1	.	.	.	.	.	.	.	.	1
Rams . .	3	.	.	.	.	.	.	.	.	3
Ewes . .	130	.	.	.	.	.	.	.	.	130
Tegs . .	85	.	.	.	.	.	.	.	.	85
Lambs . .	131	.	.	.	.	.	.	.	.	131
Pigs . .	29	.	.	.	.	.	.	.	.	29
Boar . .	1	.	.	.	.	.	.	.	.	1
Fowls . .	40	.	.	.	.	1	.	.	.	39

as they may think good, and their employers, though quite conscious of the delinquency, pass it off with the remark, "So long as the stock look well I don't interfere too much with the feeding." This attitude is hardly consistent with sound business. It is absolutely necessary on any properly conducted farm to know what the live stock are supposed to have, and to see that they get it. The margin on feeding stock is often too small to admit of any slackness in the choice and use of rations if a profit is to be made, and though it is doubtless possible to pass astonishing quantities of cake and corn through an animal, the farmer does not necessarily see his money back, either in meat or in manurial value. The disinclination to draw up proper rations and to insist on their observance is one example of the loose business

Broad Acre Farm. Week ended 11th May, 1923.

Feeding-stuffs consumed during week (lbs.)									Name of Field or Yard where consumed
Oats	Maize meal	Cotton meal	Bran	Linseed cake	Hay	Barley	Toppings	Tail wheat	
lbs.	lbs.	lbs.	lbs.	lbs.	lbs.	lbs.	lbs.	lbs.	
280	·	·	·	·	·	·	·	·	Field 3
·	·	·	·	·	·	·	·	·	,, 3
70	·	·	·	·	·	·	·	·	,, 3
·	·	·	·	·	·	·	·	·	,, 3
·	·	·	·	·	·	·	·	·	,, 5
·	112	112	112	·	896	·	·	·	,, 18
·	·	·	·	·	·	·	·	·	,, 5
·	·	·	·	156	·	·	·	·	,, 5
·	·	·	·	·	56	·	·	·	Yard
·	·	·	·	·	·	·	·	·	Field 4
·	·	·	·	·	·	·	·	·	,, 1
·	·	·	·	·	·	·	·	·	,, 1
·	·	·	·	·	·	224	224	·	,, 1
·	·	·	·	·	·	·	·	·	Yards
·	·	·	·	·	·	·	·	56	,, Poultry houses

methods too often met with in farming, which an adequate system of accounting will do much to eliminate. In no other way is it possible to feed with the maximum efficiency, or to compare the economy of rations differing in quality or quantity[1].

[1] The writer has seen as much as 14 lb. of cake per day fed to bullocks, under the impression that any money not recovered in meat would be got back in the dung—a fallacy which would speedily have been exposed by book-keeping.

Let the farmer, then, never fail to feed according to definite rations, and if his instructions are not strictly carried out the discrepancy between foods bought and foods consumed, as recorded in his books, will soon disclose the fact.

It is hardly necessary to suggest how the recording of foods can be done, as it is a very simple matter. On the previous page is a specimen of a form which has been used with success. This form serves several purposes. It acts as a record of stock born, bought, sold and died; it enables the foods consumed by the stock to be recorded, and the columns headed "Field or Yard" show whether these foods were consumed in the yards or on the fields. This latter point is of importance in the apportionment of manurial residues. In the event, too, of agricultural valuers making a distinction between the value of dung made in yards and of that from foods consumed direct on the land, as should be done, and probably will be done before long[1], a form such as this would be indispensable, whilst if a further distinction should be made one day between the manure from young stock and milking cows, and that from feeding stock, as is theoretically desirable, the value of this form for recording purposes is obvious.

Simpler forms will suggest themselves, in fact any note-book is really sufficient for the purpose of jotting down the foods consumed, but there is always an advantage to be got by using forms specially ruled to meet the needs of the individual.

On a large stock-raising farm in Lincolnshire, and also on a Warwickshire dairy farm, the writer has seen small slips in use, one for each class of stock, thus:

[1] See *Journal of the R.A.S.E.* vol. 74, p. 107.

Broad Acre Farm. Week ending 27th September, 1913.
Foods consumed by Calves.

		s.	d.
28 calves getting per day:—¼ lb.	linseed cake	1	1
½ lb.	cotton cake		10
⅛ stone	bran		7¼
¼ stone	grains		7½
		3	2

Each of these slips is totalled up every week, and
the totals can be carried forward for a period of any
length, to show the value consumed during that period.
It is an advantage to carry weekly totals forward for
at least one month before entering in the particular
account concerned so as to save a multiplicity of entries
in it, and they may even run for the whole year.

Sometimes two of these slips are used for each class
of stock, the one for foods bought and the other for foods
grown on the farm, but this is only necessary when
large quantities have to be recorded in a small space.

Home-grown foods, such as hay, straw, mangolds,
swedes, etc., are entered on the food-sheets in the same
way as are the bought foods. With regard to the pricing
of them and of such things as pasturage, however, a
little consideration is necessary.

As already stated (see p. 22) some of the American
authorities seem to favour market values, and many of
the investigations into the cost of production on the
farm which have been conducted in this country appear
to be upon the same basis, but let it be repeated here
again that to adopt the market value standard for
pricing the items in the cost of producing any article
is to render the result useless by the mixing of two
incongruous elements. When a farmer sets out to ascertain the cost of a thing, be it milk, wheat, beef, or

anything else, he must trace that cost *right through*. If milk be his object, then in order to produce it he must grow grass, cabbage, mangolds, and make hay, and so forth, and in order that he may know the cost of the milk, he must know the cost of all these foods. They are not articles which he is producing in the expectation of sale at a profit, they are merely foods to be bought and paid for, and to go through the form of marketing them to his own cows is to record a transaction which has no existence in fact. Incidentally it may be re-marked that certain home-grown crops frequently have no market value, and unless the principle of cost be rigidly adhered to, a purely arbitrary value must be assigned to them. Turnips, for example, have no market price in most places, for whilst a certain quantity may be bought by town dairymen, and the acreage coming into the market to be let for consumption on the holding by sheep may appear to be considerable, and may arouse a good deal of competition, yet the whole amount is quite negligible when contrasted with the total acreage under this crop. It is important always to price the home-grown foods at the cost of producing them, and under no consideration to be led into an attempt to assess their market values. Coming back to the food-recording sheets, the price of a home-grown food can sometimes be stated week by week, as in the case of hay; at other times, the price can only be ascertained when the food has been consumed, as with the grazing; or again, it may be possible to charge the whole cost of production of a crop to one class of stock without the necessity of weekly entries, as in the case of a field of turnips consumed by sheep. In the case of pasture land, which will in all probability be grazed by all sorts of live stock, the fields grazed are treated as one unit, and their total cost (rent, rates, labour, manure, etc.) is ascertained. When this cost comes to be divided amongst the various classes of live stock, the sheep should be the unit, and horses, bullocks, cows, etc., can each be taken as the equivalent of so many sheep. The conversion scale adopted will depend upon the class of stock grazed, but the following may serve as an example:—1 horse = 7 sheep, 1 cow or bullock = 7 sheep, 1 yearling = 3 sheep. In practice, of course, this calculation is made once only, at the end of the year, and not each week.

As to the pricing of the Purchased Foods, it is only necessary to remark that the cost of carting from the station or warehouse, to the farm (which may amount to a very considerable sum) must be added to the invoice price before making any calculations.

Manures are of two kinds, purchased and farmyard. Purchased manures are generally bought for particular crops, as, for example, basic slag for the grass, nitrate of soda for the wheat, or superphosphate for the turnips, and in such cases the invoice itself is sufficient record. When any artificial manure is bought and taken into stock for general purposes a note must be made of the quantities used from time to time on grass or crops. No special form is needed, for the farmer's note-book or diary may suffice, but the better plan is to keep a "Stock-book," showing, on the one side, all the manures purchased and, on the other, the issues from time to time. Stocks on hand can be ascertained at any moment by balancing the book. It may be noted here that a similar book may be used to record receipts and issues of Feeding-stuffs. Dung bought is treated exactly in the

o   3

34 FARM RECORDS

same way as purchased artificial, but in the case of
dung produced on the farm, it is necessary first of all
to find out its cost. The cost of farm-yard manure is,
or rather should be, the manurial value of the foods
consumed by the stock, together with the value of any
litter used. It is not the custom to take into account
the manurial value of any green crops or roots, or of
hay and straw. In the case of pasturage and fallow
crops, the bulk of which are fed off on the land, no
alteration in the customary practice is called for, as
these things have an exceedingly low manurial value
(that of a ton of turnips which would keep one sheep
for some three months being about half-a-crown) and
it goes back into the land which produced it. This does
not apply to the same extent with hay and straw, and
there is no doubt that agricultural valuation practice
ought to allow something for the residues from them.
Valuers themselves really admit the principle, for in
many districts they will dilapidate a tenant who sells
these things, though they will allow nothing to one who
feeds them.

The valuation of food residues, then, resolves itself
into a question of the manurial value of such things as
cakes, corn, meal, etc., bought, or grown, and consumed
by the stock, excluding working horses.

From the food records it is possible to see at a glance
the nature and the quantity of these foods, and their
manurial value can be calculated from Voelcker and
Hall's Tables[1]. Such tables are not yet adopted uni-
versally by agricultural valuers, but it is certain that
they soon will be, and the only other system, namely

[1] See *Journal of the R.A.S.E.* vol. 74, p. 114. Some revision of prices
must be made to bring them into accord with present-day values.

that based on the price paid for the food, is so fundamentally wrong that the farmer, in whatever district, should never think of adopting it.

Having got the total value of the food residues, that proportion of it representing foods fed direct on the grass or arable land may be charged to those accounts direct. The rest, representing food fed in yards and boxes is then charged to a Dung Account (see p. 96). By recording the number of loads, or tons, spread on the fields from time to time, it is possible to arrive at the cost per load, or per ton, of the dung produced, and whilst on the one hand the various crops can be charged with the farm-yard manure used, the farmer, on the other hand, has his attention directed to possible extravagance in feeding, and to the consideration of more economical manuring systems.

Nothing has been said about the value of the straw used for litter. This ought in strictness to be taken into account; it need not be considered a charge against the cattle, for the work they do in treading it down can be set against the benefit they derive from it as bedding, but some charge ought to be made for it against the Dung Account, so that when the dung is distributed on the various parts of the farm, arable, grass, hops, etc., each may bear its share of indebtedness to the arable land which grew the straw. On the vast majority of farms practically the whole of the dung goes on to the arable land, so that the straw comes back to the land which grew it, and therefore with a view to reducing and simplifying the work the question of the value of the straw in the dung may, perhaps, be disregarded. For strict accountancy, however, and where dung is habitually used in considerable quantities on grass-land,

CASH

Date 1923	Receipts					L.F.			
		£	s.	d.			£	s.	d.
	Brought forward						290	6	8¼
Aug. 9	4 cows sold					98	75	10	0
	54 lbs. butter @ 2s. 2d.	5	17	0					
	190 lbs. ,, @ 2s. 4d.	22	3	4		98			
							28	0	4
	30 gallons milk @ 1s. .					98	1	10	0
,, 12	1 bull					98	20	0	0
	10 steers @ £10 . .					140	100	0	0
,, 16	3578 eggs @ 1d. . .					168	14	18	2
	1 mare "Polly," 5 yrs. old					164	50	0	0
	1 pig					118	2	10	0
,, 19	Lambs sold, viz.								
	100 @ 32s. . . .	160	0	0					
	70 @ 24s. . . .	84	0	0					
	68 @ 25s. . . .	85	0	0					
						130	329	0	0

Carried forward £911 15 2¼

BOOK.

Date 1923	Payments	£	s.	d.	L.F.	£	s.	d.
	Brought forward					432	8	7½
Aug. 9	Travelling and other expenses . . .				172	5	2	0
	2 calves @ £2. 10s. . .	5	0	0	98			
	3 heifer calves @ £2. 5s. .	6	15	0				
						11	15	0
	Whips				64		8	0
,, 12	Salt for sheep . .		2	4				
	Markers for sheep . .		1	0	130			
							3	4
	Medicine for cows . .				98		3	0
,, 16	17 pigs @ 20s. . . .	17	0	0				
	8 ,, @ 23s. . . .	9	4	0	118			
						26	4	0
	Repairs to reaper . .	1	0	0				
	12 forks		15	0	180			
						1	15	0
,, 19	Seeds (crops) . . .				196	28	11	9
	Feeding stuffs, viz.,							
	Maize	92	15	0				
	Dried grains . . .	9	5	0				
	Cake and meal . .	18	18	3				
	Bran and maize . .	44	0	0				
	Calf meal . . .	1	10	0	210			
						166	8	3
	Blacksmith's account .				180	8	7	0
	Carried forward £681 5 11½							

hop-gardens and so forth, the straw in the manure ought certainly to be charged, and the cost of production, or the Tables of Voelcker and Hall already referred to, will supply the figure at which to charge it.

The record of the loads of dung spread can be kept from day to day on the labour-sheet, in fact, it must be kept on the labour-sheet where filling manure carts is made a matter of piece-work, or it can be jotted down in any note-book or diary kept by the farmer.

Only one other record remains to be kept, namely that of **cash** received and paid. This may be dealt with in any ordinary book ruled with money columns, the pages at one opening being headed respectively, "Receipts," and "Payments." Besides the cash columns, other rulings must provide for the date of each transaction and the particulars of it, whilst a small column immediately before the cash columns is necessary for entering the "Ledger Folio" of each item, that is to say, the number of the page in the Ledger where the same transaction is also recorded. (See p. 57 for further explanation[1].)

An opening in the Cash-book (taken from the accounts of a farm in the Eastern Counties) appears on pages 36, 37.

This concludes what has to be said on the subject of Farm Records. There are other matters under this head which require the attention of the farmer, milk records, for example, but these have been dealt with on many occasions and in various publications, so that they do not call for special reference here.

---

[1] The terms "Debit" and "Credit" which are applied to Receipts and Payments are not dealt with at this stage. An explanation of them will be found on p. 44.

CHAPTER IV

THE FARM DEPARTMENTS

HAVING valued his assets and arranged for the recording of his daily transactions on the farm, the next point for the farmer to decide is the number of departments into which his enterprise divides itself. At the outset it may be wise to have few accounts, for it is always possible to increase the degree of detail when experience tells what is required, and when practice has rendered the processes of recording and of analysis almost mechanical. There must, however, be accounts for each of the products of the farm, that is to say, not only for the things sold off the farm, such as milk, beef, mutton, wheat, etc., but also for the crops which are not marketed directly but which are grown to produce some of these articles. Only by such an arrangement is the farmer able to determine the cost of everything he produces.

LAND DEPARTMENTS.

(*a*) **Arable land.** There must be an account for each crop grown on the farm, to which will be charged all items of expenditure in connection with the crop, so that the cost of production may be ascertained. In the prairie farming of the newer countries this is a very simple matter, but in this country there is some difficulty in distinguishing the cost of producing the various crops in rotation. There is the question of unexhausted manurial residues, and also of the distribution of the cost of cleaning the land, which, though done for the fallow crop, benefits all the crops in the rotation. In view of the difficulty of deciding these questions, it has been suggested that particular crops should be disregarded and that the rotation should be taken as the unit for the purpose of getting the cost. This would save trouble, but on the other hand there would be the loss of valuable information. Long ago Lawes and Gilbert framed a working scale for the valuation of unexhausted manures. This has been revised on two occasions by Voelcker and Hall, and each revision has brought it nearer to an exact representation of the values. Similarly, the cost of cleaning land under fallow crops can be apportioned between them and the following crops. The total cost of cleaning can be ascertained by estimating the cost of fallowing the land in order to make it as clean as the green crop leaves it. This cost can then be charged against each crop of the rotation in proportion to the benefit it receives from the cleaning. Unexhausted benefits of cleaning would be ascertained on the same principle as unexhausted manures.

It must be clearly understood that this apportionment of the cost of cleaning involves no abandonment of the cost principle. The cost of cleaning the land is determined with absolute accuracy, and the distribution of this cost over succeeding crops by estimation, so far from introducing error into the accounts, goes to reduce the error which would arise were the apportionment not attempted. Mathematical precision in the division of the cost is of course impossible, but the want of it will do little or nothing to impair the accuracy and value of the accounts affected.

Perhaps the easiest way by which to record and to trace these apportionments of manurial residues and cleaning benefits on the arable land is by having an account for every field. Thus, on a farm where two fields were in barley, one following wheat and the other following roots, field accounts would enable the widely differing conditions as to these benefits to be recorded and passed on to the next crops, whilst at the same time the cost of growing the two fields of barley could be combined at the end of the year if desired, to show one cost for the whole barley crop on the farm. Of course, all the necessary operations can be recorded within one account for "Barley," and the number of the accounts to be opened will thereby be greatly reduced, but in practice it will be found that field accounts make for ease and accuracy, and, added to this, they have a special interest of their own. A set of field accounts kept throughout the duration of one rotation would show the ratio of the cost of production to the realised value for each field, and the farmer would gain a good idea of the relative values of his fields. Again, it is only by field accounts that the cost of ploughing and of other farm operations can be arrived at.

(b) **Grass land.** It is desirable to make a sharp distinction between meadow-land and pasture-land, and to keep a separate account for each, so that the cost of the hay crop and the cost of the grazing may each of them be determined. In many cases the debated custom of grazing and mowing the same fields in alternate years, or as required, still prevails, but even so it is necessary to have the two accounts separated.

LIVE STOCK DEPARTMENTS.

(a) **Horses.** It is necessary to open two accounts for horses, a "Stock" account, and a "Working" account. The reason for differentiating between the two accounts will presently appear (see p. 135), but briefly, the distinction is necessary to enable the farmer to calculate accurately the cost of his horse-labour. Many farmers do a little horse-dealing, or they will buy, or breed, young horses, with the intention of selling them at a profit later on. This is quite a separate branch of farming, and it is necessary to keep it entirely apart from the cost of keeping the horses for farm-work. It is immaterial in ascertaining the cost of production whether the horse-labour is performed by young horses growing into money or by aged horses, and by opening the two accounts the farmer is enabled to get from the one his profit or loss on his horse-dealing, and from the other, the cost of his horse-labour. On farms where horses are bought and worked with no intention of resale, it may be sufficient to have one account only, entitled "Working Horses."

(b) **Cattle.** The number of cattle accounts required depends upon the style of farming. Where any stock are bred there must be a "Cows" account, whilst the others that may be wanted are a "Store Cattle" account and a "Feeding Cattle" account. It will be seen presently (see p. 103) that at different periods there will be transferences of stock from one account to another. Thus, calves as they grow up will be transferred from "Cows" to "Store Cattle" whilst the "Store Cattle" in their turn may be transferred to "Feeding Cattle" or back again to "Cows" according as they are bullocks to be fatted, or heifers to come into the breeding herd.

(c) **Sheep.** The sheep accounts are arranged on somewhat similar lines. There must be a "Breeding Flock" account, including ewe lambs that are to come back into the flock, and one for the sheep being finished for the butcher.

(*d*) **Pigs** can be dealt with on most farms in one account, and the same will also be found to be the case with (*e*) **Poultry**.

MISCELLANEOUS ACCOUNTS.

Besides the accounts foregoing, others subsidiary are necessary for convenience of book-keeping.

(*a*) **Labour.** A Labour Account is necessary for the calculation of the cost of manual labour (see p. 86). The Weekly Wages payments are charged against it, and also the value of any allowances made to the men, such as cottages rent free, milk, faggots, etc. The total of this side of the account gives the total cost of the year's manual labour, and when divided by the total number of days or hours worked by the men gives the cost of one day's work, or one hour's work, and enables the proper labour charge against each department of the farm to be calculated.

(*b*) **Rent, rates, and taxes.** These also require an account to themselves. At the end of the year the balance of the account has to be split up and charged to the various land accounts (see p. 89).

(*c*) **Sundries.** Certain expenses are always occurring which cannot be charged against any particular account. Such items as the repair of farm roads, the wages of the bailiff or foreman, etc., cannot very well be analysed and they may be charged quite properly to an account entitled "Sundry expenses" or "Establishment Charges." Nothing should be included which can be put direct to any other account, and at the end of the year, when the total is ascertained, it must be shared over the productive accounts (*i.e.* stock and land accounts) in proportion to the labour charge against each, the assumption being that these accounts will have benefited from this expenditure in that ratio. Of course the subsidiary accounts will also have benefited by the establishment expenditure, but as these are ultimately balanced to the productive accounts it seems permissible to omit the step of apportioning to them their share of this item.

CHAPTER V

BOOK-KEEPING

THE way is now clear for the merely mechanical part of accounting, and it becomes necessary to explain the technical terms and processes.

The books required are known respectively as the **Journal**, the **Cash-book**, and the **Ledger**, and although in practice the use of the Journal is sometimes neglected, such a course is strongly to be deprecated.

Each page of the Journal is ruled thus:

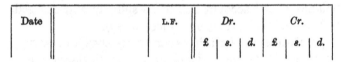

Date			L.F.	Dr.			Cr.		
				£	s.	d.	£	s.	d.

Theoretically every transaction should be entered in the Journal, and the principle upon which the entries are made is based on the fact that if one department of the farm receives value from another department, it is *debtor* to it. Thus, if the farm records show that the Wheat Account in any week has had the benefit of manual labour to the value of 25s., then the Wheat Account is said to be *debtor* to the Labour Account for this sum, and it follows, of course, that the Labour

Account is the *creditor* for a like amount. The idea is perfectly simple, and the whole principle of what is called book-keeping by double-entry depends on it.— If *A* parts with five pounds to *B*, *B* is debtor to *A*, for this sum, and *A* is *B*'s creditor for it. Here are a few transactions relating to cows taken from a farmer's records, which will serve to illustrate the process of journalising:

1922		£	s.	d.
May 1.	Valuation of cows	372	5	0
„ 28.	14 calves transferred to Store Cattle Account @ £6	84	0	0
„ 31.	Labour on cows during May . . .	1	13	0
	Purchased foods consumed by cows during May	8	3	3
	Home grown foods do.	3	6	4

The first item records the investment of a part of the farmer's capital in cows—in other words, the account for the cows has received value from the account for capital, and is therefore *debtor* to it.

The second item records the transfer of value from the Cows Account to the Store Stock Account, and the former is *credited* and the latter *debited* accordingly.

		Dr.			Cr.		
1922		£	s.	d.	£	s.	d.
May 1	Cows Dr.	372	5	0			
	To Capital Account . . .				372	5	0
	(being value of cows on hand)						
„ 28	Store Stock Dr.	84	0	0			
	To Cows				84	0	0
	(being 14 calves transferred @ £6)						
„ 31	Cows Dr.	1	13	0			
	To Labour Account . . .				1	13	0
	(being labour during May)						
	Cows Dr.	11	9	7			
	To Purchased Foods Account .				8	3	3
	„ Home-grown Foods Account .				3	6	4
	(being foods consumed during May)						

In the next transaction, the Labour Account is represented as having laid out £1. 13s. 0d. on the cows, which are therefore made *debtor* for this sum whilst the Labour Account is *creditor* for it.

Again, with the foods consumed, the food accounts are *credited* with what they have given up to the cows, and the cows are *debited* with what they have received. In this example, the transactions of the cows with the two food accounts are combined in one entry in the Journal in a manner which explains itself.

It has been said that theoretically *every* transaction on the farm should appear in the Journal, but in practice it will be found sufficient to limit the use of this book to recording those dealings where no money passes. Thus, in the examples given, the cows do not pay for the foods, neither do the store stock pay for the calves. Where money changes hands over a transaction, the record of it is made in the second of the books, namely, in the **Cash-book**. (An example of a cash-book has been given on p. 36.) The two sides of the book are headed respectively *Receipts* and *Payments*. The receipts are, of course, *debits* and the payments *credits*, for the Cash-book is simply a cash account, and it is debtor for what it receives, and creditor for what it gives away. Here are a few transactions taken from the set of accounts utilised for the Journal example:

1922		£	s.	d.
May 7	Two cows and their calves sold to Tompkins @	21	0	0
„ 11	Four ditto . . . . . . @	23	15	0
„ 16	Veterinary surgeon's account	4	17	3
„ 31	Milk sold during month	2	11	9
	Wages paid during month	15	2	9

These appear in the Cash-book thus:

Cash Book.

Dr.   Cr.

Date	Receipts	L.F.	£	s.	d.	Date	Payments	L.F.	£	s.	d.
1922						1922					
May 7	Two cows and calves @ £21		42	0	0	May 16	Veterinary surgeon's a/c (cows)		4	17	3
„ 11	Four cows and calves @ £23. 15s.		95	0	0		Wages for month		15	2	9
„ 31	Milk sales in May		2	11	9						

Obviously it is not sufficient to sort out the transactions into cash transactions and credit transactions,
and then merely to enter them into the Cash-book and
Journal respectively. In those books the only attempt
at arrangement is to follow the order of dates, and it
would be impossible to learn anything about any particular department of the farm without the tedious
process of going through both books and picking out
the items concerned. Therefore the **Ledger** is employed,
and in it all the items appearing in the Journal and
Cash-book are sorted out under their proper headings.
The work of entering up the Ledger in this way from
the Journal or Cash-book is known as "posting." The
Ledger is ruled exactly like the Cash-book, and headings
are made in it for each department of the farm, after
which the posting can begin. Taking the Journal entries
given on p. 45 and posting them into the Ledger, the
process is as follows:

"Cows Dr to Capital, £372. 5s. 0d." An account is
opened for "Capital" and it is *credited* with the sum
of £372. 5s. 0d. given up to the cows account. Then, an
account is opened for "Cows," which is *debited* with the

value it has received from the Capital Account, thus completing the "double-entry."

"Store Stock Dr to Cows £84. 0s. 0d." In this transaction the cows give up value and are *credited* with it, whilst an account opened for the "Store Stock" is the receiver and is *debited* accordingly.

"Cows Dr to Labour Account, £1. 13s. 0d." The cows have received the benefit of labour worth £1. 13s. 0d. and are *debited* with it; the Labour Account has provided the labour and is therefore *credited*.

"Cows Dr to Purchased and Home-grown Foods Accounts, £11. 9s. 7d." Again the cows are the *debtors* and the two food accounts are the *creditors*. In this case the cows are debited with the two classes of foods as a whole so as to save trouble and to reduce the number of entries. Now take the Cash-book entries, and post the Ledger from them, remembering that the Cash-book is itself nothing more than a *ledger account for the cash*, so that when the various cash items have been posted into their respective accounts in the Ledger, the double-entry is complete.

The postings to the Ledger from the Journal are given in *italics*, to distinguish them from the Cash-book items. Dealing with each item, it will be noted that on the Receipts, or debit, side of the Cash-book it is recorded that money has been received for cows and calves sold. It is not of the slightest importance to record the fact that they were sold to one Tompkins—all that is material is that the Cows Account has parted with value to the Cash Account, and that the Cash-book is to be *debited* (which has been done) and that now the Cows Account must be *credited*. In fact, in entering up the Cash-book, and in posting the Ledger from the Cash-book, the process of journalising is gone through mentally. The receipts from milk sales are dealt with in the same way. On the payments, or credit, side of the Cash-book are entries of payments to the veterinary surgeon for attendance on cows, and for general farm

Broad Acre Farm. Ledger.

Capital Account.

1922	Dr.	£	s.	d.	1922	Cr.	£	s.	d.
					May 1 By Cows . . .		372	5	0

Cows Account.

1922	Dr.	£	s.	d.	1922	Cr.	£	s.	d.
May 1	To Capital . .	372	5	0	May 28 By Store Stock . .		84	0	0
„ 31	„ Labour . .	1	13	0	„ 7 „ 2 cows and calves				
„ 31	„ Foods . . .	11	9	7	sold @ £21 . .		42	0	0
„ 16	„ Cash, veterinary				„ 11 „ 4 cows @ £23. 15s.		95	0	0
	attendance .	4	17	3	„ 31 „ milk . . .		2	11	9

Store Stock Account.

1922	Dr.	£	s.	d.	1922	Cr.	£	s.	d.
May 28	To Cows . . .	84	0	0					

Labour Account.

1922	Dr.	£	s.	d.	1922	Cr.	£	s.	d.
May 31	To cash, wages for				May 31 By Cows . . .		1	13	0
	May	15	2	9					

Purchased Foods Account.

1922	Dr.	£	s.	d.	1922	Cr.	£	s.	d.
					May 31 By Cows . . .		8	3	3

Home-grown Foods Account.

1922	Dr.	£	s.	d.	1922	Cr.	£	s.	d.
					May 31 By Cows . . .		3	6	4

N.B. In practice, of course, each account would appear on a separate page of the Ledger.

wages during the month of May. In these cases the cash account has been *credited* with the value given up, and it remains only to *debit* the Cows and Labour Accounts respectively with the values they have received. This is the whole art of "double-entry." The very expression

o

is sufficient to frighten many people, who talk of "book-keeping by double-entry" as if it were extremely difficult, whereas the process is simply the application of the commonest of common sense to the understanding of what happens when value is transferred from one part of the business to another part.

Enough should have been said to show how the items composing the farm records find their way into the departmental accounts in the Ledger; and a complete example will now be given showing twelve months accounts on a Gloucestershire farm for the year 1922–3.

The following is a statement of the Assets and Liabilities of the farmer at the beginning of the year (October 1922), together with his cash transactions, receipts and payments, month by month to the end of the year.

October 1, 1922.

Assets:			£	s.	d.
Cash in Bank			1	9	5
Horses (*at valuation*)			367	1	0
Cows and bull (*at per head*)			425	0	0
Other cattle (,,)			481	0	0
Pigs (,,)			60	0	0
Poultry (,,)			21	15	0
Wheat	1922 crop (*at cost*)		122	4	4
,,	1923 ,, (,,)		45	12	0
Barley	1922 ,, (,,)		51	14	0
,,	1923 ,, (,,)		20	4	0
Beans	1922 ,, (,,)		97	11	6
Oats	1922 ,, (,,)		192	13	3
Swedes and turnips	1922 ,, (,,)		51	11	8
Mangolds	1922 ,, (,,)		50	6	9
Potatoes	1922 ,, (,,)		45	17	4
,,	1923 ,, (,,)		38	9	4
Hay	1922 ,, (,,)		122	17	5
,,	1923 ,, (,,)		122	14	11
Pastures	(,,)		48	8	5
Implements	(*at valuation*)		229	11	6
Tools and small implements (,,)			5	11	10
Feeding stuffs (*at cost*)			42	1	10
Farmyard manure (,,)			10	10	1

	£	s.	d.
Insurance (*paid in advance*)	6	19	2
Wages (*National Health Insurance stamps on hand*)		12	6
Sundry Debtors	59	7	0

Liabilities:

	£	s.	d.
Rent owing	170	0	0
Sundry Creditors	36	10	8

RECEIPTS AND PAYMENTS.

October, 1922.

Receipts:

	£	s.	d.
In-calf heifer	37	0	0
3 calves	9	4	0
2 cows	44	5	0
1 steer	19	4	0
4 pigs	33	15	6
Half-ton potatoes	1	0	0
Milk sold last year (*see Sundry Debtors*) . .	14	12	2
Peas ,, (,,) . .	29	14	0
Cash drawn from Bank	40	0	0
,, ,, ...	31	9	4

Payments:

	£	s.	d.
Last year's Accounts (*see Sundry Creditors*) . .	31	7	2
Cash for private expenses	15	12	11
1 cow	40	0	0
Wages	31	6	0
Carriage on cow		6	6
Postages		3	4
Cheque on Bank for cash	40	0	0
,, ,, ...	31	9	4

November, 1922.

Receipts:

	£	s.	d.
1 pig	2	5	0
Apples	3	12	0
Milk	31	11	9
Cash drawn from Bank	38	18	2

Payments:

	£	s.	d.
Last year's Accounts (*see Sundry Creditors*) . .	5	3	6
Wages	42	5	0
Allowance to cowman on calf born . . .		2	0
Postages		3	2
Cheque on Bank for cash	38	18	2

December, 1922.

Receipts:	£	s.	d.
Peas sold last year (*see Sundry Debtors*) . .	7	0	0
Fruit ,, (,,) . .	8	0	10
14 qrs. wheat	30	16	0
13½ qrs. beans	32	8	0
4 pigs	30	7	0
Apples	1	16	0
Peas	1	15	0
Milk	37	18	6
Cash drawn from Bank	34	16	0

Payments:	£	s.	d.
Shorthorn Association fee		4	6
Cider-making	1	10	0
1 ton 1 cwt. sharps	11	10	0
10 cwt. bran	4	9	0
Repairs to implements		2	9
3 bushels Laxton peas (*seed*)	7	11	0
Wages	31	5	0
Insurance stamps	3	5	0
Postages		3	3½
Cheque on Bank for cash	34	16	0

January, 1923.

Receipts:	£	s.	d.
Milk	32	7	2
2 qrs. oats	3	4	0
Cash drawn from Bank	26	4	10

Payments:	£	s.	d.
Cash for private expenses	24	0	0
Half-year's rent	170	0	0
Annual subscriptions: general . . .	3	0	0
Milk Recording Society .	3	3	0
Cattle Society . . .	1	1	0
Horse Society . . .	1	1	0
Petrol		17	0
Bank Charges		9	8
Cheque book		5	0
Private insurance	3	14	9
Wages	25	0	0
Postages		1	10
Market expenses		6	0
Harness repairs		3	0
Cheque on Bank for cash	26	4	10

February, 1923.

Receipts:	£	s.	d.
Wood	2	10	0
Cash from self	5	0	0

Receipts:	£	s.	d.
1 pig	5	13	6
Milk	29	9	4
Cash drawn from Bank	21	1	11

Payments:			
Half-year's Rates	37	0	1
2 tons 1 cwt. decorticated cotton cake . . .	28	16	11
Private insurance	4	5	7
Trap and motor licences	2	5	0
Wages	20	15	0
Postages		2	4½
Telegrams and stationery		4	6
Cheque on Bank for cash	21	1	11

March, 1923.

Receipts:			
Service fee (bull)	1	8	6
Barley	1	15	0
7 store cattle	121	19	0
Milk	21	13	10
Cash drawn from Bank	35	7	2

Payments:			
Sack hire		16	8
Petrol		16	0
Cash for private expenses	36	0	0
14 bushels Lincoln peas (seed)	40	13	9
1 ton 1 cwt. sharps	9	10	9
Miscellaneous general expenses for quarter . .	2	3	6
Cash for private expenses	3	0	0
Wages	32	1	0
Allowance to cowman on calves born . . .		4	0
Postages		2	8
1 cwt. bran		8	0
Carriage on peas		2	0
Nails for fencing	1	0	4
Cheque on Bank for cash	35	7	2

April, 1923.

Receipts:			
3 horses	54	0	9
1 cow	19	14	3
Apples	2	0	0
Milk	24	11	6
20 qrs. wheat	43	0	0
Cash drawn from Bank	23	12	7

Payments:			
Water rates	8	6	0
Shoeing horses	5	6	2
Harness repairs	1	10	9

Payments: £   s.   d.
  Clover seed   8   7   2
  Mangold seed   18   6
  Wages   22   8   0
  Groom with horses   5   0
  Postages   2   3
  Allowance to cowman on calf born . . .   4   0
  Files   5   4
  Petrol   8   0
  Sack hire   16   8
  Cheque on Bank for cash 23 12   7

May, 1923.

Receipts:
  Milk   16   4   7
  Cash from self 6 16   6
  Cash drawn from Bank 34 19   5

Payments:
  Cash for private expenses 6 16   0
  Coal for threshing   12   7   6
  Wages 33 13   0
  Insurance stamps   1   0   0
  Postages   4   5
  Allowance to cowman on calf born . . .   2   0
  Cheque on Bank for cash 34 19   5

June, 1923.

Receipts:
  1 store beast   31   2   0
  1 pig   2   1   6
  1 ton mangolds   10   0
  31½ cwt. potatoes   3   5   3
  Mangolds   4   5   0
  Cash from self   11   9
  Milk 23 15   1
  Mangolds 2 19   0
  Potatoes   15   0
  Cash drawn from Bank   22   5   9

Payments:
  Wages 26 11   6
  Cash for private expenses   4   1   0
  Postages   1   9
  Allowances to cowman on calf born . .   2   0
  Castrating pigs   2   6
  Cheque on Bank for cash   22   5   9

July, 1923.

Receipts:
  Mangolds   2   0   0
  Potatoes   1   0   0

Receipts:

	£	s.	d.
Cash from self	50	0	0
1 truck mangolds	3	2	6
Milk	21	5	2
3 sacks wheat	3	9	9
Cash from self	3	17	0
Peas	9	9	0
Cash drawn from Bank	38	9	2

Payments:

Wages	42	17	6
,, cherry minding (*bird scaring*)	12	14	0
,, pea picking	6	10	10
Insurance stamps	3	0	0
Cartridges for bird scaring (*fruit*)		4	3
Postages, telegrams, stationery		14	2
Half-year's rent	170	0	0
,, rates	39	0	6
Cash for private expenses	3	0	0
Cheque on Bank for cash	38	9	2

August, 1923.

Receipts:

Peas	35	0	0
Cherries	33	6	0
Milk	18	4	8
2 cows	47	8	0
Mangolds	1	10	0
Cash drawn from Bank	19	10	10

Payments:

Postages		2	10
Wages	17	18	0
,, pea-picking	39	15	8
Miscellaneous general expenses	1	10	0
2 buckets		9	6
Fagging hooks		10	6
Cheque on Bank for cash	19	10	10

September, 1923.

Receipts:

Service fee (bull)	2	15	6
Lincoln peas	141	1	0
Milk	15	10	2
1 sack beans	1	4	0
Cash from self	50	0	0
Cash drawn from Bank	3	3	9

Payments:

2 tons sharps	18	17	8
Shoeing horses	2	14	6
Petrol	1	13	3
Miller for grinding foods	4	11	5
Cash for private expenses	24	0	0

Payments:								£	*s.*	*d.*
Water rate .	.	.	.	.	.	.	.	2	16	0
Weighing machine	.	.	.	.	.	.	.	4	15	0
Root pulper .	.	.	.	.	.	.	.	1	5	0
Threshing tackle hire	.	.	.	.	.	.	12	7	6
Insurance (Fire, etc.)	.	.	.	.	.	.	7	5	7
Wages .	.	.	.	.	.	.	.	45	2	0
Insurance stamps .	.	.	.	.	.	.	1	10	0
Postages	.	.	.	.	.	.	.		2	3
Allowance to cowman on calves born	.	.	.		9	0
Petrol .	.	.	.	.	.	.	.		3	9
Cheque on Bank for cash	.	.	.	.	.	3	3	9

It is now possible to make a start with the book-keeping, by entering all the foregoing transactions. In every-day business the practice is, of course, to enter up the Journal, Cash-book and Ledger *daily*, but to proceed in this way in a text-book example is obviously impossible. It is therefore necessary to deal first with all the *credit* transactions, by journalising them, and then with all the *cash* transactions by entering them in the Cash-book. Both Journal and Cash-book are then posted to the Ledger. To aid the reader in following up the credit and cash transactions respectively, the former are printed in *italics*, and the latter in ordinary type.

The first fact recorded is the distribution of the farmer's Capital (assets and liabilities) over the departments of the farm, by means of entries in the *Journal*. Each department is made a *debtor* to Capital for the value it may receive in the shape of the farmer's assets, and similarly each is made a *creditor* of Capital for the value it may give in the shape of the farmer's liabilities. To save the time and trouble which would be involved in making a separate Journal entry in respect of each item (such as, "Cash Dr. to Capital"; "Horses Dr. to Capital," and so on through the whole list of items) they are all combined, so far as the Capital Account is concerned, under the heading "Sundry A/cs." The figures appearing in the Ledger Folio (L.F.) column indicate the pages in Cash-book or Ledger to which the items against them are subsequently posted.

Journal (1).

1922		L.F.	Dr.			Cr.		
			£	s.	d.	£	s.	d.
Oct. 1	Sundry A/cs Dr., viz.:							
	Cash .	C.B.1	1	9	5			
	Horses	5	367	1	0			
	Cows .	8	425	0	0			
	Other cattle	7	481	0	0			
	Pigs .	9	60	0	0			
	Poultry	10	21	15	0			
	Wheat 1922 crop	12	122	4	4			
	,, 1923 ,,	12	45	12	0			
	Barley 1922 ,,	13	51	14	0			
	,, 1923 ,,	13	20	4	0			
	Beans 1922 ,,	14	97	11	6			
	Oats 1922 ,,	15	192	13	3			
	Swedes and turnips 1922 ,,	18	51	11	8			
	Mangolds 1922 ,,	19	50	6	9			
	Potatoes 1922 ,,	22	45	17	4			
	,, 1923 ,,	22	38	9	4			
	Hay 1922 ,,	11	122	17	5			
	,, 1923 ,,	11	122	14	11			
	Pastures .	20	48	8	5			
	Implements .	23	229	11	6			
	Tools and small implements	24	5	11	10			
	Feeding stuffs .	25	42	1	10			
	Farmyard manure .	33	10	10	1			
	Insurance .	26	6	19	2			
	Wages .	31		12	6			
	Sundry Debtors	3	59	7	0			
	To Capital A/c	1				2721		4
	(being assets at date)							
Oct. 1	Capital A/c Dr. .	1	206	10	8			
	To Sundry A/cs, viz.:							
	Rent .	28				170	0	0
	Sundry Creditors .	4				36	10	8
	(being liabilities at date)							

The items, for the most part, need no explanation. It will be observed that *two* departmental accounts are needed for certain crops in those cases where the items relate to the crops of different seasons. Thus, "Wheat, 1922 Crop, £122. 4s. 4d." refers to the crop in stack, harvested in the summer of 1922; whilst "Wheat, 1923 Crop, £45. 12s. 0d." refers to work done, and possibly seed sown, for the crop to be harvested in the summer of 1923. "Sundry Debtors, £59. 7s. 0d." represents the total of the amounts owing *to* the farmer by sundry persons at the end of the previous year, and by reference to the Receipts for the months of October and December it will be seen how the sum was made up, and when it was paid. Similarly "Sundry Creditors, £36. 10s. 8d." represents the total of the bills owing *by* the farmer at the end of the previous year; reference to the Payments for October and November will show when he paid them. "Rent, £170" is really in the same category, being money owing to the landlord, but it is usually set out by itself instead of running it in with other debts.

Having completed the *Journal* thus far (for there will be other items to be journalised at a later stage) the Cash-book (or cash account) must be written up. This is a very simple matter, the money for things sold and bought during the year being entered up the former on the "Receipts," or *debit* side (the cash account being the receiver of value, and therefore *debtor* to the account parting with value), the latter on the "Payments," or *credit* side (the cash account giving up value, and therefore being the *creditor* of the account receiving it). The name of the account to which each item belongs is written first, with a brief explanatory note after it. Thus, taking the record of cash receipts in October, the first items are "In-calf Heifer, £37; 3 Calves, £9. 4s.; 2 Cows, £44. 5s.; 1 Steer, £10. 4s." These were all sold on the same day. The heifer, the calves and the steer belong to the "Cattle Account," and the cows to the "Cows Account" and the receipt of money by their sale appears, accordingly, on the Receipts side (Dr.) of the Cash-book, thus:

Dr.		Bank			Cash		
Oct. 31	To Cattle A/c	65	8	0			
	In-calf heifer £37.						
	3 calves £9. 4s.						
	1 steer £19. 4s.						
	To Cows A/c	44	5	0			
	2 cows						

Similarly, taking the first item in the October payments, "Last year's accounts, £31. 7s. 2d.," this is entered on the *Payments* side (Cr.) of the Cash-book. Referring to the Cash-book (p. 61) it will be noticed that there are two money columns on each side, both for receipts and payments, one headed "*Bank*" and the other "*Cash*." This is necessary to enable the farmer to differentiate between value received, or paid, in the form of cheques and in the form of money. The former are entered in the "*Bank*" column, and the latter in the "*Cash*" column. Thus, the balance of the two "Bank" columns should always agree with the balance shown in the Bank pass-book, whilst the balance of the two "Cash" columns should always agree with the amount of cash in the office cash-box.

As in the case of the *Journal*, a "Ledger Folio" (L.F.) column is necessary on each side of the Cash-book, to give a reference to the Ledger Accounts to which the various cash items are ultimately posted. In practice, of course, this column is filled up as the work of posting the cash items into their respective Ledger Accounts proceeds.

CASH

	Receipts (Dr.)	L.F.	Bank			Cash		
1922			£	s.	d.	£	s.	d.
Oct. 1	To Cash in Bank (Capital A/c) . .	J. 1	1	9	5			
	„ Bank	con.				40	0	0
„ 31	„ Cattle A/c	7	65	8	0			
	In-calf heifer £37							
	3 calves £9. 4s.							
	1 steer £19. 4s.							
	„ Cows A/c. 2 cows	8	44	5	0			
	„ Pigs A/c. 4 pigs	9	33	15	6			
	„ Potatoes A/c. Half-ton . . .	20	1	0	0			
	„ Sundry Drs. A/c	3	44	6	2			
	Milk sold last year £14. 12s. 2d.							
	Peas „ £29. 14s.							
	„ Bank	con.				31	9	4
Nov. 30	„ Pigs A/c. 1 pig	9	2	5	0			
	„ Fruit A/c. Apples	16				3	12	0
	„ Cows A/c. Milk	8	31	11	9			
	„ Bank	con.				38	18	2
Dec. 31	„ Sundry Drs. A/c	3	15	0	10			
	Peas sold last year £7							
	Fruit „ £8. 0s. 10d.							
	„ Wheat A/c. 14 qrs.	12	30	16	0			
	„ Beans A/c. 13¼ qrs.	14	32	8	0			
	„ Pigs A/c. 4 pigs	9	30	7	0			
	„ Fruit A/c. Apples	16	1	16	0			
	„ Peas A/c	17	1	15	0			
	„ Cows A/c. Milk	8	37	18	6			
	„ Bank	con.				34	16	0
	Carried forward		374	2	2	148	15	6

BOOK.

Payments (Cr.)		L.F.	Bank			Cash		
			£	s.	d.	£	s.	d.
1922 Oct. 1	By Cash	con.	40	0	0			
„ 31	„ Sundry Crs. A/c. Last year's A/c	4	31	7	2			
	„ Private A/c. Drawings . . .	2	15	12	11			
	„ Cows A/c	8	40	6	6			
	1 cow £40							
	Carriage 6s. 6d.							
	„ Cash	con.	31	9	4			
	„ Wages A/c	31				31	6	0
	„ Establishment A/c. Postages . .	29					3	4
Nov. 30	„ Sundry Crs. A/c. Last year's A/c .	4	5	3	6			
	„ Wages A/c	31				42	5	0
	„ Cattle A/c. Allowance (calf) . .	7					2	0
	„ Establishment A/c. Postages . .	29					3	2
	„ Cash	con.	38	18	2			
Dec. 31	„ Cows A/c. Shorthorn Assoc. Fee .	8		4	6			
	„ Sundries A/c. Cider-making . .	30	1	10	0			
	„ Feeding Stuffs A/c	25	15	19	0			
	1 ton 1 cwt. Sharps £11. 10s.							
	10 cwt. bran £4. 9s.							
	„ Implements A/c. Repairs . .	23					2	9
	„ Seed A/c. 3 bushels Laxton Peas .	27	7	11	0			
	„ Wages A/c	31				34	10	0
	Wages £31. 5s.							
	Nation Health In-							
	surance Stamps £3. 5s.							
	„ Establishment A/c. Postages . .	29					3	3½
	„ Cash	con.	34	16	0			
	Carried forward		262	18	1	108	15	6½

CASH BOOK

	Receipts (*Dr.*)	L.F.	Bank	Cash
			£ s. d.	£ s. d.
1923	*Brought forward*		374 2 2	148 15 6
Jan. 31	To Cows A/c. Milk	8	32 7 2	
	„ Oats A/c. 2 qrs.	15	3 4 0	
	„ Bank	con.		26 4 10
Feb. 28	„ Sundries A/c. Wood	30	2 10 0	
	„ Private A/c	2	5 0 0	
	„ Pigs A/c. 1 pig	9	5 13 6	
	„ Cows A/c. Milk	8	29 9 4	
	„ Bank	con.		21 1 11
	Carried forward		452 6 2	196 2 3

(continued).

		L.F.	Bank			Cash		
	Payments (Cr.)		£	s.	d.	£	s.	d.
1923	Brought forward		262	18	1	108	15	6½
Jan. 31	By Private A/c	2	27	14	9			
	Drawings £24							
	Insurance £3. 14s. 9d.							
	„ Rent, rates and taxes A/c Half-year's Rent	28	170	0	0			
	„ Establishment A/c	29	3	14	8	1	4	10
	Subscription £3							
	Petrol 17s.							
	Bank Charges 9s. 8d.							
	Cheque Book 5s.							
	Postages 1s. 10d.							
	Market expenses 6s.							
	„ Cows A/c	8	4	4	0			
	Subscription to Milk Recording Society £3. 3s.							
	Subscription £1. 1s.							
	„ Horses (W) A/c	6	1	4	0			
	Subscription £1. 1s.							
	Harness repairs 3s.							
	„ Wages A/c	31				25	0	0
	„ Cash	con.	26	4	10			
Feb. 28	„ Rent, Rates and Taxes A/c Half-year's Rates	28	37	0	1			
	„ Feeding Stuffs A/c 2 tons 1 cwt. decorticated cotton cake	25	28	16	11			
	„ Private A/c. Insurance . . .	2						
	„ Establishment A/c	29	4	5	7			
	Trap and Motor Licences £2. 5s.		2	5	0		6	10½
	Postages 2s. 4½d.							
	Telegrams and stationery 4s. 6d.							
	„ Wages A/c	31				20	15	0
	„ Cash	con.	21	1	11			
	Carried forward		589	9	10	156	2	3

CASH BOOK

	Receipts (*Dr.*)	L.F.	Bank £	s.	d.	Cash £	s.	d.
1923 Mar. 31	*Brought forward*		452	6	2	196	2	3
	To Cows A/c	8	23	2	4			
	Milk £21. 13s. 10d.							
	Service Fee (bull) £1. 8s. 6d.							
	„ Barley A/c	13	1	15	0			
	„ Cattle A/c. 7 stores	7	121	19	0			
	„ Bank	con.				35	7	2
Apr. 30	„ Horses (S) A/c. 3 horses . . .	5	54	0	9			
	„ Cows A/c	8	44	5	9			
	1 cow £19. 14s. 3d.							
	Milk £24. 11s. 6d.							
	„ Fruit A/c. Apples	16	2	0	0			
	„ Wheat A/c. 20 qrs.	12	43	0	0			
	„ Bank	con.				23	12	7
	Carried forward		742	9	0	255	2	0

(continued).

	Payments (*Cr.*)	L.F.	Bank			Cash		
			£	*s.*	*d.*	£	*s.*	*d.*
1923	*Brought forward*		589	9	10	156	2	3
Mar. 31	By Granary A/c. Sack hire . . .	22		16	8			
	,, Establishment A/c	29				3	2	2
	Petrol 16*s.*							
	Miscellaneous expenses £2. 3*s.* 6*d.*							
	Postages 2*s.* 8*d.*							
	,, Private A/c. Drawings . . .	2	39	0	0			
	,, Seed A/c. 14 bushels Lincoln Peas							
	and Carriage 2*s.*	27	40	15	9			
	,, Feeding Stuffs A/c	25	9	18	9			
	1 ton 1 cwt. Sharps £9. 10*s.* 9*d.*							
	1 cwt. bran 8*s.*							
	,, Wages A/c	31				32	1	0
	,, Cattle A/c. Allowance on calves .	7					4	0
	,, Fences A/c. Nails	32	1	0	4			
	,, Cash	con.	35	7	2			
Apr. 30	,, Rent, Rates and Taxes A/c Water Rate	28	8	6	0			
	,, Horses (W) A/c)	6	6	16	11		5	0
	Shoeing £5. 6*s.* 2*d.*							
	Harness repairs £1. 10*s.* 9*d.*							
	Groom's Fee 5*s.*							
	,, Seed A/c	27	9	5	8			
	Clover seed £8. 7*s.* 2*d.*							
	Mangold seed 18*s.* 6*d.*							
	,, Wages A/c	31				22	8	0
	,, Establishment A/c . . .	29					10	3
	Postages 2*s.* 3*d.*							
	Petrol 8*s.*							
	,, Cattle A/c. Allowance on calves .	7					4	0
	,, Tools A/c. Files	24					5	4
	,, Granary A/c. Sack hire . . .	22		16	8			
	,, Cash	con.	23	12	7			
	Carried forward		765	6	4	215	2	0

o

CASH BOOK

	Receipts (Dr.)	L.F.	Bank			Cash		
			£	s.	d.	£	s.	d.
1923	Brought forward		742	9	0	255	2	0
May 31	To Cows A/c. Milk	8	16	4	7			
	,, Private A/c	2	6	16	6			
	,, Bank	con.				34	19	5
June 30	,, Cattle A/c. 1 store beast . . .	7	31	2	0			
	,, Pigs A/c. 1 pig	9	2	1	6			
	,, Mangolds A/c	19	7	14	0			
	,, Potatoes A/c. 37½ cwt. . . .	20				4	0	3
	,, Private A/c	2					11	9
	,, Cows A/c. Milk	8	23	15	1			
	,, Bank	con.				22	5	9
July 31	,, Mangolds A/c	19	5	2	6			
	,, Potatoes A/c	20				1	0	0
	,, Private A/c	2	50	0	0	3	17	0
	,, Cows A/c. Milk	8	21	5	2			
	,, Wheat A/c. 3 sacks . . .	12				3	9	9
	,, Peas A/c	17	9	9	0			
	,, Bank	con.				38	9	2
	Carried forward		915	19	4	363	15	1

(continued).

	Payments (Cr.)	L.F.	Bank			Cash		
			£	s.	d.	£	s.	d.
1923	*Brought forward*		765	6	4	215	2	0
May 31	By Private A/c. Drawings . . .	2	6	16	0			
	„ Granary A/c. Coal for threshing .	22	12	7	6			
	„ Wages A/c	31				34	13	0
	Wages £33. 13s.							
	National Health In-							
	surance Stamps £1							
	„ Establishment A/c. Postages . .	29					4	5
	„ Cattle A/c. Allowance on calf. .	7					2	0
	„ Cash	con.	34	19	5			
June 30	„ Private A/c. Drawings . . .	2	4	1	0			
	„ Wages A/c	31				26	11	6
	„ Establishment A/c. Postages . .	29					1	9
	„ Cattle A/c. Allowance on calf .	7					2	0
	„ Pigs A/c. Castrating	9					2	6
	„ Cash	con.	22	5	9			
July 31	„ Fruit A/c. Cartridges (bird scaring)	16					4	3
	„ Establishment A/c. Postages, tele-							
	grams, stationery	29					14	2
	„ Rent, Rates and Taxes A/c . .	28	209	0	6			
	Half-year's rent £170							
	„ rates £39. 0s. 6d.							
	„ Private A/c. Drawings . . .	2	3	0	0			
	„ Wages A/c	31	19	4	10	45	17	6
	Wages £42. 17s. 6d.							
	National Health In-							
	surance Stamps £3							
	Cherry minding £12. 14s.							
	Pea picking £6. 10s. 10d.							
	„ Cash	con.	38	9	2			
	Carried forward		1115	10	6	323	15	1

CASH BOOK

	Receipts (*Dr.*)	L.F.	Bank			Cash		
			£	s.	d.	£	s.	d.
1923	*Brought forward*		915	19	4	363	15	1
Aug. 31	To Peas A/c	17	35	0	0			
	„ Fruit A/c. Cherries	16	33	6	0			
	„ Cows A/c	8	65	12	8			
	C cows £47. 8s.							
	Milk £18. 4s. 8d.							
	„ Bank	con.				19	10	10
	„ Mangolds A/c	19	1	10	0			
Sept. 30	„ Cows A/c	8	15	10	2	2	15	6
	Milk £15. 10s. 2d.							
	Service Fee £2. 15s. 6d.							
	„ Peas A/c. Lincoln peas . . .	17	141	1	0			
	„ Beans A/c. 1 sack . . .	14				1	4	0
	„ Private A/c	2	50	0	0			
	„ Bank	con.				3	3	9
	„ Balance—Bank overdraft—Carried							
	forward		1	11	3			
			1259	10	5	390	9	2

(continued).

	Payments (Cr.)	L.F.	Bank			Cash		
			£	s.	d.	£	s.	d
1923	*Brought forward*		1115	10	6	323	15	1
Aug. 31	By Tools A/c	24	1	0	0			
	2 buckets 9s. 6d.							
	Fagging hooks 10s. 6d.							
	,, Establishment A/c . . .	29				1	12	10
	Postages 2s. 10d.							
	Miscellaneous general							
	expenses £1. 10s.							
	,, Wages A/c	31	39	15	8	17	18	0
	Pea picking £39. 15s. 8d.							
	Wages £17. 18s.							
	,, Cash	con.	19	10	10			
Sept. 30	,, Feeding Stuffs A/c . . .	25	23	9	1			
	2 tons Sharps £18. 17s. 8d.							
	Grinding foods £4. 11s. 5d.							
	,, Horses (W) Shoeing . . .	6	2	14	6			
	,, Establishment A/c . . .	29	9	2	7	2	3	
	Petrol £1. 17s.							
	Insurance Premiums £7. 5s. 7d.							
	Postages 2s. 3d.							
	,, Private A/c. Drawings . .	2	24	0	0			
	,, Rent, Rates and Taxes A/c. Water							
	Rate	28	2	16	0			
	,, Implements A/c	23	6	0	0			
	Weighing Machine £4. 15s.							
	Root pulper £1. 5s.							
	,, Granary A/c. Threshing tackle hire	22	12	7	6			
	,, Wages A/c	31				46	12	0
	Wages £45. 2s.							
	National Health In-							
	surance Stamps £1. 10s.							
	,, Cattle A/c. Allowance on calves .	7				9	0	
	,, Cash	con.	3	3	9			
			1259	10	5	390	9	2
	By Balance—Bank overdraft—Brought							
	forward		1	11	3			

The Cash-book is so straightforward and simple that the work it involves requires but little further explanation. Dealing, first, with the *Receipts*, the first item "Oct. 1 To Cash in Bank (Capital a/c) £1. 9s. 5d." represents the bank-balance at the end of the previous year, which appears in the statement of Assets given in the *Journal* (p. 57). Hence the reference in the Ledger Folio column "J 1." The second item, "To Bank, £40," in which the money appears in the *Cash column*, represents a cheque drawn and cashed to replenish the Office Cash-box, and so to enable the farmer to make payments of wages, and other expenses, in cash. This is not a real receipt, as it is balanced (as will be noted) by a payment of £40 entered in the *Bank column* on the *Payments* side of the Cash-book. It is a *payment* as regards the Bank column and a *receipt* as regards the Cash column. Thus, the reference in the "Ledger Folio" column is "contra" (abbreviated to "con.") and indicates that the item is posted not in some Leger Account, as would be the case if it were a *bona-fide* receipt or payment, but on the *contra* side of the Cash-book. Similar transactions occur throughout the year.

The next item in the *Receipts* requiring explanation appears under date, Feb. 28—"Private a/c, £5." This represents £5 paid by the farmer from his private purse into the farm bank account, and credit will be given to him for this in a *Private Account* in the Ledger (p. 75). Other transactions of the same character occur from time to time.

Nothing else arises on the *Receipts* side of the Cash-book until the end of the year. The last item "Sept. 30. By Balance—Bank overdraft—carried forward, £1. 11s. 3d.," is the amount that has to be added to the *Receipts* to make the two Bank columns agree, and reference to the Bank Pass-book will show that the Bank Account is overdrawn to this extent. Had there been a balance in the bank, instead of an overdraft, the total Bank payments would have been less than the total Bank receipts, and an amount equal to the balance in the Bank Pass-book would have had to be added to the *Payments* side of the Cash-book to make the Bank columns agree.

Dealing now with the *Payments*, the first item "Oct. 1. By Cash, £40," the amount being entered in the Bank column, has really been explained already. It represents a cheque drawn on the Bank account, and cashed, and paid into the Cash column on the *Receipts* side, to enable the farmer to make money payments. Similar transactions occur at intervals.

"Oct. 31. Private a/c, Drawings, £15. 17s. 11d." represents a cheque drawn on the farm Bank Account for the farmer's private expenditure. The amount is subsequently debited (charged) against him in his *Private Account* in the Ledger (p. 75).

"Oct. 31. Establishment a/c, Postages, 3s. 4d." The *Establishment Account* is an account opened in the Ledger for sundry items of general expenditure connected with the management of the farm (see, for example, items on *Payments* side of the Cash-book for Establishment a/c under date Jan. 31 and Feb. 28).

Nothing further seems to call for comment. It remains only to say that every care must be used, in writing up the Cash-book, to see that each item is debited or credited to its appropriate account. As the main object of the book-keeping is to ascertain the costs in every department of the farm, all entries must be made with this in mind. Nor must anything be charged to *Establishment a/c* or to *Miscellaneous Expenses* until it is beyond doubt that a direct allocation to one of the departmental accounts is impossible.

The next stage in the work is to post all the *Journal* and *Cash-book* entries into the Ledger in order of dates. (In practice it is probable that all these transactions would be posted from day-to-day). The Ledger is a book ruled so that the double page will take both debit and credit entries, the former being made on the left hand, and the latter on the right hand. The first step is to "open accounts" in the Ledger for every department of the farm by inscribing the name of each at the top of a page. In this example the necessary accounts are:

General Accounts	*Live Stock Accounts*	*Land Accounts*
Capital	Horses (stock)	Wheat
Private	Horses (working)	Barley
Sundry Debtors	Cattle	Beans
Sundry Creditors	Cows	Peas
Hay	Pigs	Oats
Feeding stuffs	Poultry	Fruit
Granary		Swedes and turnips
Seed		Mangolds
Farmyard manure		Potatoes
Implements		Pastures
Tools		
Insurance		
Rent, rates and taxes		
Wages		
Fences		
Establishment		
Sundries		

The work of posting can then proceed. Taking the first *Journal* entry, "Oct. 1. Sundry a/cs Dr. to Capital a/c £2721. 4*s*. 3*d*." the Capital Account is *credited* with £2721. 4*s*. 3*d*., and each of the accounts composing the item "Sundry a/cs" is debited with its share. On the credit side of the Capital account there appears the entry "By Sundry a/cs £2721. 4s. 3d.," whilst on the debit side of the Horses (Stock) Account there appears the entry "To Capital a/c £367. 1s. 0d.," and so on through all the items. The use of the "Ledger Folio" column is now apparent, for it supplies the reference from one account to the other one jointly concerned in the transaction. In the example given the *accounts* have been numbered in place of the folios, because it is necessary to print more than one account on each page.

The posting from the Journal to the Ledger is so simple that no further explanations should be needed, except in the case of the item "Cash in Bank, £1. 9s. 5d." on Oct. 1. This is not entered in any Ledger account, for it has already been entered in the Cash-book (see p. 60), which is nothing other than a ledger account for cash, kept in a separate book for the sake of convenience, on account of the multiplicity of the entries to be made in it.

The cash items are easily and quickly posted to the Ledger when this fact is remembered, for it is only necessary to carry each purchase, or sale, to its appropriate Ledger account and *to the other side of it*. Thus, taking the third item on the *Receipts* side of the Cash-book—"Oct. 31. To Cattle a/c, £65. 8s." Cash having been *debited* with value received from the Cattle Account, the Cattle Account must be *credited* with the value surrendered to Cash, and there will be an entry in the Cattle Account accordingly (p. 77) "Oct. 31. By Cash a/c, £65. 8s."

LED

Capital

		Dr.				£	s.	d.	£	s.	d.
1922											
Oct. 1		To Sundry A/cs	.	.	J. 1	206	10	8			

Private

							£	s.	d.	£	s.	d.
1922												
Oct. 1	To Cash A/c	.	.	.	C.B. 1	15	12	11			
1923												
Jan. 31	,,	,,	.	.	,, 2	27	14	9			
Feb. 28	,,	,,	.	.	,, 2	4	5	7			
Mar. 31	,,	,,	.	.	,, 3	39	0	0			
May 31	,,	,,	.	.	,, 4	6	16	0			
June 30	,,	,,	.	.	,, 4	4	1	0			
July 31	,,	,,	.	.	,, 4	3	0	0			
Sept. 30	,,	,,	.	.	,, 5	24	0	0			

Sundry Debtors

						£	s.	d.	£	s.	d.
1922											
Oct. 1	To Capital A/c	.	.	J. 1	59	7	0			

Sundry Creditors

						£	s.	d.	£	s.	d.
1922											
Oct. 31	To Cash A/c	.	.	C.B. 1	31	7	2			
Nov. 30	,,	,,	.	.	,, 1	5	3	6			

Horses (Stock)

					£	s.	d.	£	s.	d.
1922										
Oct. 1	To Capital A/c	.	J. 1	367	1	0			

Horses (Working)

						£	s.	d.	£	s.	d.
1923											
Jan. 31	To Cash A/c	.	.	C.B. 2	1	4	0			
Apr. 30	,,	,,	.	.	,, 3	6	16	11			
	,,	,,	.	.	,, 3		5	0			
Sept. 30	,,	,,	.	.	,, 5	2	14	6			

GER.

Account No. 1.

	Cr.		£	s.	d.	£	s.	d.
1922 Oct. 1	*By Sundry A/cs* . .	*J. 1*	2721	4	3			

Account No. 2.

			£	s.	d.
1923 Feb. 28	By Cash A/c . . .	C.B. 2	5	0	0
May 31	,, ,, . . .	,, 4	6	16	6
June 30	,, ,, . . .	,, 4		11	9
July 31	,, ,, . . .	,, 4	50	0	0
	,, ,, . . .	,, 4	3	17	0
Sept. 30	,, ,, . . .	,, 5	50	0	0

Account No. 3.

			£	s.	d.
1922 Oct. 31	By Cash A/c . . .	C.B. 1	44	6	2
Dec. 31	,, ,, . . .	,, 1	15	0	10

Account No. 4.

			£	s.	d.
1922 Oct. 1	*By Capital A/c* . .	*J. 1*	36	10	8

Account No. 5.

			£	s.	d.
1923 Apr. 30	By Cash A/c . .	C.B. 3	54	0	9

Account No. 6.

Cattle

	Dr.			£	s.	d.	£	s.	d.
1922									
Oct. 1	To Capital A/c	. .	J. 1	481	0	0			
Nov. 30	,, Cash A/c	. .	C.B. 1		2	0			
1923									
Mar. 31	,, ,,	. . .	,, 3		4	0			
Apr. 30	,, ,,	. . .	,, 3		4	0			
May 31	,, ,,	. . .	,, 4		2	0			
June 30	,, ,,	. . .	,, 4		2	0			
Sept. 30	,, ,,	. . .	,, 5		9	0			

Cows

	Dr.			£	s.	d.	£	s.	d.
1922									
Oct. 1	To Capital A/c	. .	J. 1	425	0	0			
,, 31	,, Cash A/c	. .	C.B. 1	40	6	6			
Dec. 31	,, ,,	. . .	,, 1		4	6			
1923									
Jan. 31	,, ,,	. . .	,, 2	4	4	0			

Pigs

	Dr.			£	s.	d.	£	s.	d.
1922									
Oct. 1	To Capital A/c	. .	J. 1	60	0	0			
1923									
June 30	,, Cash A/c .	. .	C.B. 4		2	6			

Poultry

	Dr.			£	s.	d.	£	s.	d.
1922									
Oct. 1	To Capital A/c	. .	J. 1	21	15	0			

Hay

	Dr.			1922 Crop			1923 Crop		
1922									
Oct. 1	To Capital A/c	. .	J. 1	122	17	5	122	14	11

Account No. 7.

	Cr.			£	s.	d.	£	s.	d.
1922									
Oct. 31	By Cash A/c .	. .	C.B. 1	65	8	0			
1923									
Mar. 31	,, ,,	. . .	,, 3	121	19	0			
June 30	,, ,,	. . .	,, 4	31	2	0			

Account No. 8.

				£	s.	d.	
1922							
Oct. 31	By Cash A/c .	. .	C.B. 1	44	5	0	
Nov. 30	,, ,,	. . .	,, 1	31	11	9	
Dec. 31	,, ,,	. . .	,, 1	37	18	6	
1923							
Jan. 31	,, ,,	. . .	,, 2	32	7	2	
Feb. 28	,, ,,	. . .	,, 2	29	9	4	
Mar. 31	,, ,,	. . .	,, 3	23	2	4	
Apr. 30	,, ,,	. . .	,, 3	44	5	9	
May 31	,, ,,	. . .	,, 4	16	4	7	
June 30	,, ,,	. . .	,, 4	23	15	1	
July 31	,, ,,	. . .	,, 4	21	5	2	
Aug. 31	,, ,,	. . .	,, 5	65	12	8	
Sept. 30	,, ,,	. . .	,, 5	15	10	2	
	,, ,,	. . .	,, 5	2	15	6	

Account No. 9.

				£	s.	d.	
1922							
Oct. 31	By Cash A/c .	. .	C.B. 1	33	15	6	
Nov. 30	,, ,,	. . .	,, 1	2	5	0	
Dec. 31	,, ,,	. . .	,, 1	30	7	0	
1923							
Feb. 28	,, ,,	. . .	,, 2	5	13	6	
June 30	,, ,,	. . .	,, 4	2	1	6	

Account No. 10.

Account No. 11.

Wheat

	Dr.		£ s. d.	£ s. d.
1922 Oct. 1	*To Capital A/c* . .	*J. 1*	1922 Crop *122 4 4*	1923 Crop *45 12 0*

Barley

1922 Oct. 1	*To Capital A/c* . .	*J. 1*	1922 Crop *51 14 0*	1923 Crop *20 4 0*

Beans

1922 Oct. 1	*To Capital A/c* . .	*J. 1*	1922 Crop *97 11 6*	

Oats

1922 Oct. 1	*To Capital A/c* . .	*J. 1*	1922 Crop *192 13 3*	

Fruit

1923 July 31	To Cash A/c . . .	C.B. 4	4 3	

Peas

Swedes and Turnips

1922 Oct. 1	*To Capital A/c* . .	*J. 1*	1922 Crop *51 11 8*	

Account No. 12.

						£	s.	d.	£	s.	d.
1922						1922 Crop					
Dec. 31	By Cash A/o .	.	.	C.B. 1		30	16	0			
1923											
Apr. 30	,,	,,	.	.	.	,, 3	43	0	0		
July 31	,,	,,	.	.	.	,, 4	3	9	9		

Account No. 13.

						£	s.	d.
1923						1922 Crop		
Mar. 31	By Cash A/o .	.	.	C.B. 3		1	15	0

Account No. 14.

						£	s.	d.
1922						1922 Crop		
Dec. 31	By Cash A/o .	.	.	C.B. 1		32	8	0
1923								
Sept. 30	,,	,,	.	.	.	,, 5	1	4	0

Account No. 15.

						£	s.	d.
1923						1922 Crop		
Jan. 31	By Cash A/o .	.	.	C.B. 2		3	4	0

Account No. 16.

						£	s.	d.
1922								
Nov. 30	By Cash A/o .	.	.	C.B. 1		3	12	0
Dec. 31	,,	,,	.	.	.	,, 1	1	16	0
1923								
Apr. 30	,,	,,	.	.	.	,, 3	2	0	0
Aug. 31	,,	,,	.	.	.	,, 5	33	6	0

Account No. 17.

						£	s.	d.
1922								
Dec. 31	By Cash A/o .	.	.	C.B. 1		1	15	0
1923								
July 31	,,	,,	.	.	.	,, 4	9	9	0
Aug. 31	,,	,,	.	.	.	,, 5	35	0	0
Sept. 30	,,	,,	.	.	.	,, 5	141	1	0

Account, No. 18.

Mangolds

	Dr.		£ s. d.	£ s. d.
1922 Oct. 1	To Capital A/c . .	J. 1	1922 Crop 50 6 9	

Potatoes

			£ s. d.	£ s. d.
1922 Oct. 1	To Capital A/c . .	J. 1	1922 Crop 45 17 4	1923 Crop 38 9 4

Pastures

			£ s. d.	
1922 Oct. 1	To Capital A/c .	J. 1	48 8 5	

Granary

			£ s. d.	
1923 Mar. 31	To Cash A/c . . .	C.B. 3	16 8	
Apr. 30	,, ,, . .	,, 3	16 8	
May 31	,, ,, . .	,, 4	12 7 6	
Sept. 30	,, ,, . .	,, 5	12 7 6	

Implements

			£ s. d.	
1922 Oct. 1	To Capital A/c . .	J. 1	229 11 6	
Dec. 31	,, Cash A/c . .	C.B. 1	2 9	
1923 Sept. 30	,, ,, . .	,, 5	6 0 0	

Tools and Small

			£ s. d.	
1922 Oct. 1	To Capital A/c . .	J. 1	5 11 10	
1923 Apr. 30	,, Cash A/c . . .	C.B. 3	5 4	
Aug. 31	,, ,, . . .	,, 5	1 0 0	

Feeding Stuffs

			£ s. d.	
1922 Oct. 1	To Capital A/c . .	J. 1	42 1 10	
Dec. 31	,, Cash A/c . . .	C.B. 1	15 19 0	
1923 Feb. 28	,, ,, . . .	,, 2	28 16 11	
Mar. 41	,, ,, . . .	,, 3	9 18 9	
Sept. 30	,, ,, . . .	,, 5	23 9 1	

Account No. 19.

	Cr.			£	s.	d.	£	s.	d.
1923				1922 Crop					
June 30	By Cash A/c . . .	C.B. 4		7	14	0			
July 31	,, ,, . . .	,, 4		5	2	6			
Aug. 31	,, ,, . . .	,, 5		1	10	0			

Account No. 20.

				£	s.	d.	£	s.	d.
1922				1922 Crop					
Oct. 31	By Cash A/c . . .	C.B. 1		1	0	0			
1923									
June 30	,, ,, . . .	,, 4		4	0	3			
July 31	,, ,, . . .	,, 4		1	0	0			

Account No. 21.

Account No. 22.

Account No. 23.

Implements Account No. 24.

Account No. 25.

o

6

Insurance

	Dr.			£	s.	d.	£	s.	d.
1922									
Oct. 1	*To Capital A/c* . .		*J. 1*	6	19	2			

Seed

	Dr.			£	s.	d.	£	s.	d.
1922									
Dec. 31	To Cash A/c . . .		C.B. 1	7	11	0			
1923									
Mar. 31	,, ,, . .		,, 3	40	15	9			
Apr. 30	,, ,, . . .		,, 3	9	5	8			

Rent, Rates and Taxes

	Dr.			£	s.	d.	£	s.	d.
1923									
Jan. 31	To Cash A/c . . .		C.B. 2	170	0	0			
Feb. 28	,, ,, . . .		,, 2	37	0	1			
Apr. 30	,, ,, . . .		,, 3	8	6	0			
July 31	,, ,, . . .		,, 4	209	0	6			
Sept. 30	,, ,, . . .		,, 5	2	16	0			

Establishment

	Dr.			£	s.	d.	£	s.	d.
1922									
Oct. 31	To Cash A/c . . .		C.B. 1		3	4			
Nov. 30	,, ,, . . .		,, 1		3	2			
Dec. 31	,, ,, . . .		,, 2		3	3½			
1923									
Jan. 31	,, ,, . . .		,, 2	3	14	8			
	,, ,, . . .		,, 2	1	4	10			
Feb. 28	,, ,, . . .		,, 2	2	5	0			
	,, ,, . . .		,, 2		6	10½			
Mar. 31	,, ,, . . .		,, 3	3	2	2			
Apr. 30	,, ,, . . .		,, 3		10	3			
May 31	,, ,, . . .		,, 4		4	5			
June 30	,, ,, . . .		,, 4		1	9			
July 31	,, ,, . . .		,, 4		14	2			
Aug. 31	,, ,, . . .		,, 5	1	12	10			
Sept. 30	,, ,, . . .		,, 5	9	2	7			
	,, ,, . . .		,, 5		2	3			

Sundries

	Dr.			£	s.	d.	£	s.	d.
1922									
Dec. 31	To Cash A/c . .		C.B. 1	1	10	0			

Account No. 26.

	Cr.		£ s. d.	£ s. d.

Account No. 27.

Account No. 28.

1922 Oct. 1	By Capital A/c . .	J. 1	170 0 0	

Account No. 29.

Account No. 30.

1923 Feb. 28	By Cash A/c . . .	C.B. 2	2 10 0	

Wages

	Dr.			£	s.	d.	£	s.	d.
1922									
Oct. 1	To Capital A/c . .	J. 1			12	6			
,, 31	,, Cash A/c . . .	C.B. 1		31	6	0			
Nov. 30	,, ,, . . .	,, 1		42	5	0			
Dec. 31	,, ,, . . .	,, 1		34	10	0			
1923									
Jan. 31	,, ,, . . .	,, 2		25	0	0			
Feb. 28	,, ,, . . .	,, 2		20	15	0			
Mar. 31	,, ,, . . .	,, 3		32	1	0			
Apr. 30	,, ,, . . .	,, 3		22	8	0			
May 31	,, ,, . . .	,, 4		34	13	0			
June 30	,, ,, . . .	,, 4		26	11	6			
July 31	,, ,, . . .	,, 4		19	4	10			
	,, ,, . . .	,, 4		45	17	6			
Aug. 31	,, ,, . . .	,, 5		39	15	8			
	,, ,, . . .	,, 5		17	18	0			
Sept. 30	,, ,, . . .	,, 5		46	12	0			

Fences

			£	s.	d.
1923					
Mar. 31	To Cash A/c . . .	C.B. 3	1	0	4

Farmyard Manure

			£	s.	d.
1922					
Oct. 1	To Capital A/c . .	J. 1	10	10	1

Account No. 31.

	Cr.		£ s. d.	£ s. d.

Account No. 32.

Account No. 33.

CHAPTER VI

CLOSING THE ACCOUNTS

THE way is now clear for making the final apportionments of charges and credits, as between one account and another, and for closing the year's books. The order in which this work is done is material, for it is obvious that accounts for labour, rent, food-stuffs, etc., must be closed by crediting them, and debiting the departments with which they have been concerned, before such accounts as those for corn or cattle can be closed.

The Wages Account (No. 31) should be the first one taken in hand. As it appeared when it was left (p. 85) it contained charges for Insurance Stamps on hand at the beginning of the year, and for the monthly cash payments for wages throughout the year. But the labour on the farm costs more than this, seeing that some of the men have had certain allowances, *i.e.* cottages free of rent, and a milk allowance in one case, in addition to their cash wages. It is necessary, therefore, to charge the Wages Account with the value of these items, and to credit the Rent Account (No. 28) and the Cows Account (No. 8) at the same time. This is done by making a record in the *Journal* (see below), and then posting the items to the *Ledger Accounts* concerned (see Wages Account, p. 130; Rent Account, p. 129; Cows Account, p. 115). The total cost of the labour of the farm for the year is thus ascertained, and a reference to the account shows that it amounts to £455. 19*s.* This has to be distributed over the various departments of the farm in which the labour has been applied. Reference to the Labour-sheets shows that part of the work has been of the nature of piece-work, and done at special rates for particular accounts. This is all summarised and an appropriate entry made in the *Journal* (see below) by which the accounts concerned are each of them *debited*, and the Wages Account *credited* with the amounts involved. The *Ledger* is then posted from the *Journal*, with the result that Wages Account (No. 31, p. 131) is credited with £116. 2*s*. 9*d*., and ten other accounts are debited with various sums making up this total. There is then left in the Wages Account a balance of £339. 16*s*. 3*s*. One pound of this represents Insurance Stamps on hand at the end of the year, and this is credited to the account and carried forward to the debit of the next year, leaving the sum of £338. 16*s*. 3*d*. as representing the cost of the ordinary labour on the farm.

Reference to the Labour Analysis Sheets (p. 26) shows that this is the cost of 12,510 hours of labour spent in thirty-five different departments of the farm. The hours spent in these departments are recorded, so that it is a matter of simple arithmetic to find out the labour charge against each of them. Once more the *Journal* is called into use to record this apportionment, and the various *Ledger Accounts* are then posted from it. All these Journal entries for closing the Labour Account and apportioning the labour charges to the various departments of the farm appear as follows:

Journal (2).

		L.F.	Dr. £ s. d.	Cr. £ s. d.
Wages A/c	Dr.	31	16 9 0	
To Sundry A/cs viz.:				
Rent (for cottages)		28		15 12 0
Cows (for milk)		8		17 0
Allowances to men				
Sundry A/cs	Dr.			
Viz.: Granary 1922		22	3 15 0	
Wheat 1923		12	7 14 2	
Barley ,, ...		13	1 13 9	
Beans ,, ...		14	5 16 3	
Oats ,, ...		15	2 12 5	
Mangolds ,, ...		19	6 13 6	
Peas ,, ...		17	52 13 11	
Hay ,, ...		11	19 5 6	
Fruit ,, ...		16	12 14 0	
Potatoes 1922		20	3 4 3	
To Wages A/c		31		116 2 9
Special rates, piece-work etc. directly chargeable as above				
Sundry A/cs	Dr.			
Viz.: Cows 2747 hours		8	74 7 11	
Cattle 1299 ,,		7	35 3 7	
Pigs 306 ,,		9	8 5 9	
Horses (Working) 1242½ ,,		6	33 13 1	
,, (Stock) 77½ ,,		5	2 2 0	
Fences 367 ,,		32	9 18 9	
Establishment 563 ,,		29	15 5 0	
Implements 60½ ,,		23	1 12 9	
Granary 1922 64½ ,,		22	1 14 11	
Seed 1 ,,		27	7	
Farmyard manure 76 ,,		33	2 1 2	
Feeding Stuffs 22½ ,,		25	12 3	
Granary 1923 37 ,,		22	1 0 0	

Journal (3).

				L.F.	Dr.			Cr.		
					£	s.	d.	£	s.	d.
Barley	1922	18	hours	13		9	9			
,,	1923	158	,,	13	4	5	7			
,,	1924	35	,,	13		19	0			
Beans	1922	44	,,	14	1	3	10			
,,	1923	631	,,	14	17	1	9			
Wheat	1922	160	,,	12	4	6	8			
,,	1923	656½	,,	12	17	15	7			
,,	1924	45	,,	12	1	4	5			
Oats	1922	155½	,,	15	4	4	3			
,,	1923	268½	,,	15	7	5	5			
,,	1924	103	,,	15	2	15	10			
Potatoes	1922	547	,,	20	14	16	3			
,,	1923	196	,,	20	5	6	2			
Fruit		5½	,,	16		3	0			
Hay	1922	23	,,	11		12	5			
,,	1923	662	,,	11	17	18	7			
Swedes and turnips	1922	157½	,,	18	4	5	4			
Mangolds	1922	504	,,	19	13	13	0			
,,	1923	357	,,	19	9	13	5			
Peas	,,	693½	,,	17	18	15	7			
Straw	,,	14	,,	35		7	7			
Pastures		212½	,,	21	5	15	1			
To Wages A/c				31				338	16	3
Being 12,510 hours worked @ 6·5d. per hour										

A reference to the Wages Account (No. 31, p. 130) will show how it appears when balanced off in this way.

The account next in order for closing is Rent, Rates and Taxes (No. 28). In this case half-a-year's rent is owing to the landlord, and it is necessary, therefore, to debit the account with this sum; the total then stands at £597. 2s. 7d. (see p. 128). This, however, includes *three* half-year's rents, as a half-year owing at the beginning of the year has been paid and charged on Jan. 31. Allowing for this, and for the rents of cottages already credited to this account and charged to Wages Account, there remains a balance of £411. 10s. 7d. This is found to represent 53s. 1d. per acre, and this amount has to be charged against every field according to its size, and the total credited to the Rent, etc. Account. Once more an entry in the *Journal* is made, setting forth this transaction, and the *Ledger Accounts* concerned are then posted from it.

Journal (4).

				L.F.	Dr.			Cr.		
					£	s.	d.	£	s.	d.
Sundry A/cs			*Dr.*							
Viz.: *Wheat*	*1923*	*15*	*acres*	*12*	*39*	*16*	*3*			
Barley	,,	*5*	,,	*13*	*13*	*5*	*5*			
Oats	,,	*6*	,,	*15*	*15*	*18*	*6*			
Beans	,,	*7*	,,	*14*	*18*	*11*	*7*			
Peas	,,	*6*	,,	*17*	*15*	*18*	*6*			
Potatoes	,,	*9*	,,	*20*	*2*	*13*	*1*			
Mangolds	,,	*1½*	,,	*19*	*3*	*19*	*7*			
Swedes	,,	*1¼*	,,	*18*	*3*	*19*	*8*			
Hay	,,	*20*	,,	*11*	*74*	*6*	*4*			
Fruit	,,	*5*	,,	*16*	*13*	*5*	*5*			
Pastures	,,	*79*	,,	*21*	*209*	*16*	*3*			
To Rent, Rates and Taxes A/c			.	*28*				*411*	*10*	*7*
Apportionment at 53s. 1d. per acre										

The Rent, etc. Account is then ruled off, and the amount of the half-year's rent owing is carried down to start the next year's account.

Next in order of closing stand the accounts for Sundry Debtors (No. 3) and Sundry Creditors (No. 4). At the end of the financial year there must always be accounts owing to and by the farmer, in respect of sales and purchases by him; these must be brought into account, first, by *debiting* the Sundry Debtors Account with the items due to the farmer and crediting the departments from which the sales were effected; and second, by *crediting* the Sundry Creditors Account with the items due by the farmer and debiting the departments for which the purchases were made. The process goes, first of all, through the *Journal* in the following form:

Journal (4).

	L.F.	Dr. £ s. d.	Cr. £ s. d.
Sundry Debtors A/c Dr.	3	34 14 10	
To Sundry A/cs			
Viz.: Cows milk	8		15 19 2
Wheat 1922	12		2 10 0
Fruit	16		3 0 8
Swedes 1922	18		12 0 0
Mangolds 1922	19		1 5 0
Debtors at close of year			
Sundry A/cs Dr.			
Viz.: Establishment	29	3 16 10½	
Horses (W). Shoeing and			
harness repairs . .	6	4 7 1	
Cattle. Veterinary Surgeon .	7	2 13 6	
To Sundry Creditors A/c . . .	4		10 17 5½
Creditors at date			

The *Ledger* is then posted.

One small difficulty in connection with farm costing is illustrated by the next operation. A certain number of days of horse-labour have been spent on two or three accounts which are themselves contributory to the cost of horse-labour. Oats, for example, employ horse-labour and are themselves an item in the cost of it. The occurrence of such cases depends, in a measure, on the date on which the books are closed, but when they arise they must be dealt with by assuming a figure for the cost of the horse-days spent, and debiting the accounts concerned and crediting the Horses (Working) Account. Usually the items themselves are few in number, and the number of days of horse-labour are few likewise.

Moreover, the error in estimating the cost of the horse-day should be inconsiderable if the figure is based on the calculated figures of previous years.

In this case, an assumption of cost must be made in respect of work done by horses for the Implement Account (No. 23); the Granary, 1922, Account (No. 22); the Wheat, 1922, Account (No. 12); and the Oats, 1922, Account (No. 15). These accounts are debited with an estimated cost at the rate of 11*d.* per hour, which proved to be within ·3*d.* of the actual cost, and the Horses (Working) Account is credited (see Journal (5) below). The figures are then posted to the respective Ledger Accounts.

The completion of this transaction makes it possible to close the Granary Account (No. 22). This is the account which has been charged with all the stacking, thatching, threshing and delivery expenses in connection with the corn crops, and it is necessary, now, to *charge* these accounts with the total expenditure, *pro rata*, and to *credit* the Granary Account, which then balances and can be ruled off (see, first, *Journal* (5) on p. 93 and then *Ledger* Accounts Nos. 12, 15, 14, 13 and 22 on pp. 116–121, 124). The Home-grown Foods Account (No. 34) can now be dealt with. Certain crops have been fed to the farm live-stock, and their cost is *credited* to the respective crop accounts, and *debited* to the Home-grown Foods Account (see Journal (5) below, and the appropriate Ledger Accounts). One further item remains to be charged against the Home-grown Foods Account, namely the cost of grinding some of the corn. This has been done whilst preparing purchased feeding-stuffs, so that the Purchased Feeding-stuffs Account (No. 25) must be *credited* with the cost, and the Home-grown Feeding Stuffs *debited*. (See Journal (5) below).

Journal (5).

	L.F.	Dr. £	Dr. s.	Dr. d.	Cr. £	Cr. s.	Cr. d.
Sundry A/cs Dr.							
Viz.: *Implements*	23		7	0			
Granary 1922	22	1	3	10			
Wheat ,, ...	12		11	0			
Oats ,, ...	15		12	11			
To *Horses (Working) A/c* . . .	6					2 14	9
Estimated cost of horse-labour							
@ 11d.							
Sundry 1922 A/cs Dr.							
Viz.: *Wheat*	12	15	10	0			
Oats	15	10	10	2			
Beans	14	5	10	4			
Barley	13	1	11	7			
To *Granary 1922 A/c*	22					33 2	1
1922 Costs transferred							
Home-grown Foods A/c Dr.	34	339	2	5			
To *Sundry A/cs*							
Viz.: *Hay* 1922 41 tons . .	11				123	9	10
Wheat ,, 49 cwt. . .	12				26	4	5
Oats ,, 145 ,, . .	15				161	11	8
Barley ,, 14½ ,, . .	13				27	16	6
For Foods fed to Stock							
Home-grown Foods A/c Dr.	34	4	11	5			
To *Feeding Stuffs A/c*	25					4 11	5
Grinding foods							

The charge against the various departments of the farm for depreciation on Implements used is now calculated. It is got from the Implements Stock-book, which has been described already (see p. 14). The depreciation shown therein on implements for general use (carts, etc.) is charged against the Establishment Account (No. 29); on those for the various classes of live-stock, to their respective accounts; on arable land implements, to arable crops on the basis of horse-labour; performed on those for meadow or grass-land, to those accounts (see Journal (6) below). When the figures in the Journal have been posted to the appropriate Ledger Accounts, the Implements Account (No. 23, p. 124) can be closed and ruled off, for the balance which it shows represents the value of implements on hand, and this figure is carried forward to start the account for the following year.

The Small Tools are also depreciated (see Account, No. 24, p. 126), by writing off about 20 per cent. of the cost, and this amount is charged against the Establishment Account, as no more detailed apportionment of this item is practicable. The percentage deducted for depreciation represents about a five-years' life, which is quite long enough for articles which include such perishable things as hay forks, brooms, etc. (see Journal (6) below, and Ledger Accounts). The Small Tools Account is then balanced, the balance representing the value of stock on hand, and closed. The straw must now be transferred from the various crop accounts to the debit of the Straw Account (No. 35, p. 132). See Journal (6) below.

The way is now clear for the important operation of closing the Horses (Working) Account (No. 6, p.   ). It is complete except for charging the home-grown foods and purchased foods consumed; the straw used; the summer grazing and the depreciation on the horses. These figures are obtained from the records already described, and after making the entry in the *Journal* (see below), they are posted to the *Ledger*. The balance of the Horses (Working) Account, £187. 8s. 11d., represents the cost of the horse-labour for the year in doing 3981 hours work, and it is apportioned amongst the various departments of the farm for which horse-work has beén done according to the time worked in each. The operation is recorded in the *Journal* (see (6) and (7) below), and the many *Ledger* accounts are then charged and the Horses (Working) Account credited. This account now balances and is ruled off.

Journal (6).

	L.F.	Dr.			Cr.		
		£	s.	d.	£	s.	d.
Sundry A/cs Dr.							
Viz.: Establishment	29	11	11	4			
Cattle	7	1	5	11			
Horses (Working)	6	1	13	7			
Poultry	10		8	1			
Pigs	9		1	7			
Cows	8	1	7	7			
Beans 1923	14	1	4	3			
Wheat ,, ...	12	1	3	9			
,, 1924	12		1	5			
Peas 1923	17	1	6	5			
Barley ,, ...	13		8	7			
,, 1924	13		1	4			
Oats 1923	15		16	8			
,, 1924	15		3	9			
Swedes 1923	18		4	2			
Mangolds ,, ...	19		4	2			
Potatoes ,, ...	20		18	9			
Hay ,, ...	11	1	12	1			
Pastures	21		8	1			
To Implements A/c	23				25	1	6
Depreciation, repairs, etc. and labour written off							
Establishment A/c Dr.	29	1	7	8			
To Tools A/c	24				1	7	8
Depreciation written off							
Straw A/c Dr.	35	57	15	4			
To sundry 1922 A/cs							
Viz.: Wheat 15 tons, 18 cwt. 56 lbs. .	12				20	7	5
Barley 2 tons, 2 cwt. . . .	13				7	13	7
Oats 13 tons, 18 cwt. . .	15				29	14	4
Straw from crops							

The other live-stock accounts have now to be charged with the purchased and home-grown foods consumed

by them, and then to be credited with the manurial
values of some of these foods. The entries in the *Journal*
giving effect to these things will be found below, and,
when the *Ledger* has been posted the Feeding Stuffs
Account (No. 25, p. 126) and the Home-grown Foods
Account (No. 34, p. 132) can be closed, carrying forward
the stock of feeding stuffs on hand to the debit of the
accounts for the next year.

Journal (7).

			L.F.	Dr.			Cr.		
				£	s.	d.	£	s.	d.
Horses (*Working*) A/c		Dr.	6	139	9	6			
To Sundry A/cs									
Viz.: Home-grown Foods									
Hay £26. 0s. 10d. }			34				76	3	6
Oats £50. 2s. 8d. }									
Straw			35				3	1	4
Feeding Stuffs—Bran . . .			25				4	5	0
Pastures			21				32	4	7
Horses (*Stock*) A/c—Depreciation			5				23	15	1
For sundry charges									
Sundry A/cs		Dr.							
Viz.: Cows	1	hour	8			11			
Pigs	6	hours	9		5	8			
Cattle	121½	,,	7	5	14	5			
Fences	10	,,	32		9	5			
Establishment	60	,,	7	2	16	10			
Granary 1923	19¼	,,	22		18	4			
Seed	1	,,	27			11			
Farmyard Manure	120	,,	33	5	13	0			
Feeding Stuffs	27	,,	25	1	5	5			
Straw 1923	20	,,	35		18	10			
Potatoes 1922	20	,,	20		18	10			
,, 1923	174	,,	20	8	3	11			
Swedes 1922	3	,,	18		2	10			
Mangolds ,,	236½	,,	19	11	2	8			
,, 1923	240½	,,	19	11	6	5			
Fruit	3½	,,	16		3	3			
Hay 1923	509	,,	11	23	19	3			
Peas ,,	601	,,	17	28	5	11			
Wheat ,,	584½	,,	12	27	10	5			
,, 1924	45	,,	12	2	2	4			
Barley 1923	209½	,,	13	9	17	3			
,, 1924	57	,,	13	2	13	6			
Beans 1923	490	,,	14	23	1	5			

Journal (8).

	L.F.	Dr.			Cr.		
		£	s.	d.	£	s.	d.
Oats 1923 279 hours . . .	15	13	2	10			
„ 1924 133¼ „ . . .	15	6	5	10			
Pastures 9 „ . . .	21		8	6			
To *Horses (Working) A/c* . . .	6				187	8	11
3981 hours worked at 11s. 3d. per hour							
Sundry A/cs Dr.							
Cows	8	57	19	9			
Pigs	9	43	15	11			
To *Feeding Stuffs A/c*	25				101	15	8
Purchased foods consumed							
Sundry Stock A/cs Dr.							
Cows	8	121	10	7			
Cattle	7	80	4	9			
Horses (Stock)	5	7	2	8			
Pigs	9	38	19	0			
Poultry	10	19	13	4			
To *Home-grown Foods A/c* . . .	34				267	10	4
Hay, oats, barley, wheat consumed							
Sundry A/cs Dr.							
Farmyard Manure	33	20	9	6			
Pastures	21	10	1	0			
To *Sundry A/cs*							
Cows	8				22	15	0
Pigs	9				7	15	6
Manurial residues of foods consumed							

The Straw Account (No. 35, p. 132) must now be finished off. It has been charged with the labour on the straw produced on the farm, and some of this has been used for thatching, and is charged to the Granary Account, 1923 (No. 22, p. 124); some has been fed to cattle and cows, and is charged to these accounts (Nos. 7 and 8, pp. 112–115); and some has been used for litter, and is charged to the Farmyard Manure Account (No. 33, p. 130). An entry in the *Journal* (see (9) below) pre-

o

cedes the posting of the various Ledger accounts, and the Straw Account is then balanced and ruled off. The balance 4s. 9d. represents the cost of the straw on hand, and this is carried forward to the debit of the account for the next year.

Journal (9).

	L.F.	Dr.			Cr.		
		£	s.	d.	£	s.	d.
Sundry A/cs Dr.							
Viz.: Granary 1923	22	3	0	8			
Cattle	7	18	7	5			
Cows	8	18	11	4			
Farmyard Manure	33	15	16	3			
To Straw A/c	36				55	15	8
For thatching, litter and feed							

The various root accounts should be closed next. Dealing first with Swedes, 1922 (No. 18, p. 122) and Mangolds, 1922 (No. 19, p. 122) it is found that certain of the cultivations and of the manure costs have to be carried forward to the crop following these roots, namely oats, 1923 (No. 15, p. 120), following the principles already described (see p. 39). Oats are *debited*, and the two root crops *credited*. The balance of the two accounts represents the cost of swedes and mangolds fed to cows, cattle and pigs, and then their accounts are therefore *debited*, and the Swedes and Mangolds Accounts credited, after which they can be cast up, and ruled off. The only other coot crop is potatoes, 1922. Some of the value of the manures applied to this is unexhausted by it, and must be *credited* to it, and debited to the crops which will follow in 1923, namely mangolds and swedes. The balance of the Potatoes, 1922, Account (No. 20, p. 123) represents the cost of potatoes fed to pigs, and their account (No. 9, p. 114) is *debited* with the amount, £26. 15s. 8d., and the potatoes are credited. The Potato Account can then be ruled off. All these transactions appear in the Journal (9) as follows:

Journal (9).

	L.F.	Dr.			Cr.		
		£	s.	d.	£	s.	d.
Oats A/c 1923 Dr.	15	28	16	7			
To Sundry A/cs viz.:							
Swedes 1922	18				15	0	2
Mangolds 1922	19				13	16	5
Cleaning cultivations and residues of manure							
Sundry A/cs Dr.							
Viz.: Cows	8	31	9	9			
Cattle	7	24	6	9			
Pigs	9		12	6			
To Sundry A/cs viz.:							
Mangolds 1922	19				32	10	10
Swedes ,, ...	18				23	18	2
Roots consumed							
Sundry A/cs Dr.							
Viz.: Mangolds 1923	19	1	15	1			
Swedes ,, ...	18	1	15	1			
To Potatoes 1922	20				3	10	2
Residues of manure							
Pigs A/c Dr.	9	26	15	8			
To Potatoes A/c	20				26	15	8
Potatoes fed to pigs							

The general expenses of the farm can now be dealt with. These are comprised in what is called the Establishment Account (No. 29, p. 128). Before the total can be distributed over the various productive accounts which may be held to have benefited by this general expenditure, the account must be completed by charging it with two further items, insurance premiums (see Account No. 26, p. 127) and the cost of maintenance of

fences (see Account No. 32, p. 131). It is then complete, and shows a total of £76. 16s. 11½d. Of this
amount, £7. 5s. 7d., represents insurance premiums paid
in advance and belonging to next year's accounts. The
Insurance Account is therefore *debited* with this sum,
and the balance, £69. 11s. 4½d., is split up between the
various crops and live-stock accounts of the farm, upon
the basis of the labour expended during the year in
each (see p. 43). The *Journal* entries necessary to
record these internal transactions appear below (Journal
(10)), and the various *Ledger* accounts concerned are
then posted.

Journal (10).

	L.F.	Dr.			Cr.		
		£	s.	d.	£	s.	d.
Establishment A/c　　　　　　*Dr.*	29	18	7	8			
To Sundry A/cs viz.:							
Insurance　.　.　.　.	26				6	19	2
Fences　.　.　.　.	32				11	8	6
Charges to be apportioned							
Sundry A/cs　　　　　　*Dr.*							
Viz.: Insurance (premium in advance)	26	7	5	7			
Cattle　.　.　.　.　.	7	8	4	4			
Cows　.　.　.　.　.	8	17	3	7½			
Pigs　.　.　.　.　.	9	1	18	0			
Hay　1923　.　.　.　.	11	8	10	3			
Wheat　1922　.　.　.	12		19	6			
,,　　1923　.　.　.	12	5	17	4			
,,　　1924　.　.　.	12		5	9			
Barley　1923　.　.　.	13	1	7	7			
,,　　1924　.　.　.	13		4	7			
Beans　1922　.　.　.	14		5	9			
,,　　1923　.　.　.	14	3	18	3			
Oats　1922　.　.　.	15		19	6			
,,　　1923　.　.　.	15	2	4	10			
,,　　1924　.　.　.	15		12	8			
Fruit　.　.　.　.	16	2	18	8			
Peas　1923　.　.　.	17	14	0	9			
To Establishment A/c　.　.　.	29				76	16	11½
Insurance premium paid in advance and apportionment of general charges							

The closing of the Farmyard Manure Account (No. 33, p. 130) follows. A certain number of loads has been recorded as being spread for the Beans, 1923 Crop (Account No. 14, p. 118), and the Peas, 1923 Crop (Account No. 17, p. 120); these are *debited* and the Farmyard Manure Account *credited*.

Journal (10).

	L.F.	Dr.			Cr.		
		£	s.	d.	£	s.	d.
Sundry A/cs Dr.							
Viz.: Beans 1923	14	16	17	1			
Peas „	17	14	9	4			
To Farmyard Manure A/c . . .	33				31	6	5
Manure applied							

The balance of the Farmyard Manure Account, £23. 3s. 7d., represents the cost of the manure still unapplied at the end of the year, and this is carried forward to the *debit* of next year, and the account is then ruled off.

During the year a certain amount of seeds have been purchased for the farm, in addition to the home-grown seed-corn used. All bought seeds have been charged against a Seed Account (No. 27, p. 126), and these have now to be *credited* to this account, and *debited* to the crop accounts concerned. In this case seed was purchased and used for the pea crop, the temporary grass for mowing in 1924, and the mangold crop. The home-grown seeds used do not require an entry in the *Journal* as they are merely *contra* items from the account for one year against that of the next.

The Pastures Account (No. 21, p. 124) can now be taken in hand. It is charged, first of all, with a small sum being the estimated cost of the aftermath of the meadow-land, which has been grazed by horses, and then the total cost of the year's grazing, £210. 5s. 1d., is apportioned amongst the various live-stock accounts upon the basis previously described (see p. 33).

The *Journal* entries appropriate to the foregoing transactions are given below (Journal (11)). After posting the *Ledger*, the Seeds and the Pastures Accounts can be closed. The Hay Account (No. 11, p. 116) can also be closed, carrying forward to the following year the cost of seed, sowing, and unexhausted residues of manures and cleaning cultivations.

Journal (11).

	L.F.	Dr.			Cr.		
		£	s.	d.	£	s.	d.
Sundry A/cs Dr.							
Viz.: Peas 1923	17	48	8	3			
Hay 1924	11	8	7	2			
Mangolds 1923	19		18	6			
To Seed A/c	27				57	13	11
Purchased seed planted							
Pastures A/c Dr.	21	2	1	4			
To Hay 1923 A/c	11				2	1	4
Aftermath grazed							
Sundry Stock A/cs Dr.							
Viz.: Horses (Stock)	5	20	1	4			
Cows	8	62	6	0			
Cattle	7	124	16	2			
Pigs	9	3	1	7			
To Pastures A/c	21				210	5	1
Apportionment of grazing costs							

The various crop accounts can now be closed. There are certain items of cost represented by unexhausted manures and cleaning cultivations which have, first, to be *credited* to the crops of the year, and *debited* to those which will follow in the next year, and when this has been done (see Journal (11) below), the various crop accounts in the *Ledger* can be balanced. The balances of the 1922 crops represent the profits made, or the losses sustained on those accounts; the balances of the 1923 crops represent the cost of those accounts up to the date of closing the books, and they are carried forward to the *debit* of the next year's accounts.

Journal (11).

	L.F.	Dr.			Cr.		
		£	s.	d.	£	s.	d.
Peas 1924 A/c Dr.	17	3	7	6			
To Wheat 1923 A/c	12				3	7	6
Cleaning cultivations taken forward (last year)							
Wheat 1924 A/c Dr.	12		5 12	4			
To Beans 1923 A/c	14					5 12	4
Residues of manure							
Hay 1924 A/c Dr.	11	15	5	5			
To Oats 1923 A/c	15				15	5	5
Cost of sowing seed 17s. 2d.							
Cleaning cultivations £14. 8s. 3d.							
Swedes 1923 A/c Dr.	18	7	8	0			
To Mangolds 1923 A/c	19				7	8	0
Labour, horse-labour, etc.							

Only three transfers remain to be made. The Cattle Account (No. 7, p. 112) must be *charged* with the cost of milk fed to calves, and the Cows Account (No. 8, p. 115) must be *credited*; and Cattle must also be *charged* with the value of calves born, and Cows *credited*.

All the eggs and poultry produced on the farm have been consumed in the farmer's household: it is therefore necessary to *charge* the Private Account (No. 2, p. 110) with their value, and to *credit* the Poultry Account (No. 10, p. 117).

The Journal entries needed for these transfers, before the *Ledger* can be posted, are as follows:

Journal (12).

	L.F.	Dr.			Cr.		
		£	s.	d.	£	s.	d.
Cattle A/c Dr.	7	67	16	6			
To Cows A/c	8				67	16	6
Milk fed to calves during the year							
Cattle A/c Dr.	7	15	0	0			
To Cows A/c	8				15	0	0
Value of calves born and transferred							
Private A/c Dr.	2	20	16	5			
To Poultry A/c	10				20	16	5
Eggs and birds consumed							

All the internal transactions are now complete. The next step is to *credit* the accounts with all valuations and to balance and close them. In the case of the 1922 crop accounts, there are no valuations, and the balances represent the profits or losses on the realisations of the crops (see, for example, Beans Account, 1922, No. 14, p. 118 "By Profit and Loss a/c £49. 17*s.* 3*d.*"). In the case of the 1923 and 1924 crops the valuations are the respective costs at the date of closing. These accounts are therefore balanced, by *crediting* them with these figures, and then carrying the balance forward to the *debit* of the new year's accounts (see Beans Account, 1923, No. 14, p. 119 "By Cost to date, c/d, £102. 0*s.* 5*d.*"). This system of valuation has the advantage, already noted, that it avoids all estimated values, and the actual cost to the farmer is carried forward until it can be compared with values realised.

The method of ascertaining the valuation figures for live-stock has already been described (see p. 9). When the live-stock accounts have been *credited* with them they are balanced off, and the balances represent the profits or losses on the respective accounts. The amounts of valuations, representing as they do the value of live-stock on hand at the close of the year, are carried forward to the *debit* of the next year's accounts (see, for example, Cows Account, No. 8, p. 114, "To Profit and Loss a/c, £45. 18s. 2½d."; and "By Stock on hand, c/d, £390. 0s. 0d.").

Implements Account, No. 23, and Tools Account, No. 24, are balanced in the same way as the live-stock accounts. Sundries Account, No. 30, is balanced by carrying the difference to Profit and Loss, and it will then be found that all the remaining accounts, such as Wages, Establishment, Pastures, etc. have either been balanced off already in the earlier stages, or else that they require only casting up, and ruling off, to complete them.

It remains only to deal with the Profit and Loss Account (No. 36, p. 132), the Private Account (No. 2, p. 110) and the Balance Sheet (p. 132).

The Profit and Loss Account is simply one in which the various profits made or losses sustained during the year, in the various departments of the farm, are collected together so that they may be seen at a glance, and so that the net result of them all may be apparent. It is an ordinary Ledger Account, and it is posted from two entries made in the *Journal*, in which it is made *debtor* to the various departments showing *losses*; whilst it is creditor to those showing gains:

Journal (12).

	L.F.	Dr.			Cr.		
		£	s.	d.	£	s.	d.
Profit and Loss A/c *Dr.*	36	386	12	1			
To Sundry A/cs							
Horses (Stock)	5				79	15	11
Cattle	7				157	7	4
Pigs	9				40	0	2
Wheat	12				3	4	11
Barley	13				5	0	3
Beans	14				49	17	3
Oats	15				4	9	1
Peas	17				6	13	8
Swedes and turnips . . .	18				5	1	6
Mangolds	19				13	3	8
Potatoes	20				21	18	4
Losses transferred							
Sundry A/cs *Dr.*							
Cows	8	45	18	2½			
Fruit	16	14	6	1			
Sundries	30	1	0	0			
To Profit and Loss A/c . . .	36				61	4	3½
Gains transferred							

On balancing the Profit and Loss Account it appears that the losses exceed the profits by £325. 7s. 9½d., and the destination of the balance of this account, whether it be a profit, as is usual, or a loss, as in this instance must be considered. If it be a profit, it represents money, or value, which the farmer is entitled to apply to his own purposes; in fact, it is probable that he will have been drawing money from the farm bank account during the year in anticipation of a profit, as happened in this case (see Private Account, No. 2, p. 110). In such instances the profit balance is carried to the Private Account, an entry being made in the Journal, first of all, by which the Private Account is *credited*, and the Profit and Loss Account *debited* with the amount. At first sight it might be supposed that the Private Account *receives,* and should consequently be *debited,* but a little consideration will make it obvious that there is no transfer of value to the Private Account; the profits made are in the form of cash in the bank, or an increase of live or dead stock on the farm, and they are *due* to the Private Account, which is therefore *creditor.* It is when the farmer draws money from the bank for his personal use that the Private Account *receives* value, and it then becomes *debtor* to the Cash Account which gives up value.

Sometimes it happens that the farmer is building up his business out of profits, and that he does not intend to draw out the profit made. In such instances it is usual to carry the profit balance to the credit of the Capital Account, as it is obvious that the capital invested in the farm is increased by the amount of the profit left in it.

In the example under consideration, however, there has been a loss. This must be dealt with in one of the two ways indicated for dealing with a profit balance; it must be carried to the farmer's Private Account, showing him as a *debtor* to the farm; or it must be carried to the *debit* of the Capital Account, thus reducing the amount of the money shown to be invested in the farm. The former method is preferable if the loss is due to exceptional circumstances, and is likely to be wiped out by profits in subsequent years. The latter method is the only sound practice if there is little likelihood of a recovery of the loss; the value has gone, and the sooner it is written off in the books the better. A third alternative is to carry the loss forward to the debit of

the next year's Profit and Loss Account. This also
should only be done when there is an expectation of
early profits to wipe it out.

In the present example it was decided to carry the
loss on the year's working to the Private Account, and
the following entry was made in the *Journal*, from which
the two Ledger accounts were posted:

Journal (13).

	L.F.	Dr.			Cr.		
		£	s.	d.	£	s.	d.
Private A/c Dr.	2	325	7	9½			
To Profit and Loss A/c . . .	36				325	7	9½
Loss for the year transferred							

The Profit and Loss Account now balances, and can
be ruled off. The Private Account shows a balance due
by the farmer to the farm of £354. 9s. 2½d. The account
is *credited* with this balance, which is carried forward to
the *debit* of the account for the following year, and it
is then cast up and closed.

There remains only the *Balance Sheet* (see p. 132).
This consists of a statement of the liabilities and of the
assets of the business. The liabilities are the moneys
put into the farm; these include the capital invested in
it by the farmer, the money owing by him to sundry
creditors and to the landlord for rent, and the money
owing to the bank for the overdraft. The assets are
the money, or money's worth possessed by the farm,
and it is obvious that this must be sufficient to balance
the liabilities. In this case the assets are represented
by the farmer's own debt to the business, the money
owing to it by sundry debtors, the value of the live and
dead stock on the farm, and small sums for Insurance

premiums for the following year, paid in advance, and for National Health Insurance Stamps on hand at the close of the financial year.

This concludes the accounts, and in their final completed form they appear as set out in the following pages.

Capital

	Dr.		L.F.	£	s.	d.	£	s.	d.
1922									
Oct. 1	To Sundry A/cs . . .		J. 1	206	10	8			
	„ Balance . . .		c/d	2514	13	7			
				2721	4	3			

Private

			L.F.	£	s.	d.	£	s.	d.
1922									
Oct. 1	To Cash A/c . . .		C.B. 1	15	12	11			
1923									
Jan. 31	„ „ . . .		„ 2	27	14	9			
Feb. 28	„ „ . . .		„ 2	4	5	7			
Mar. 31	„ „ . . .		„ 3	39	0	0			
May 31	„ „ . . .		„ 4	6	16	0			
June 30	„ „ . . .		„ 4	4	1	0			
July 31	„ „ . . .		„ 4	3	0	0			
Sept. 30	„ „ . . .		„ 5	24	0	0			
	„ Poultry A/c . . .		J. 12	20	16	5			
	„ Profit and Loss A/c . .		„ 13	325	7	9½			
				470	14	5½			
	To Balance . . .		b/d	354	9	2¼			

Sundry Debtors

			L.F.	£	s.	d.	£	s.	d.
1922									
Oct. 1	To Capital A/c . . .		J. 1	59	7	0			
1923									
Sept. 30	„ Sundry A/cs . . .		„ 4	34	14	10			
				94	1	10			
	To Balance . . .		b/d	34	14	10			

Sundry Creditors

			L.F.	£	s.	d.	£	s.	d.
1922									
Oct. 31	To Cash A/c . . .		C.B. 1	31	7	2			
Nov. 30	„ „ . . .		„ 1	5	3	6			
1923									
Sept. 30	„ Balance . . .		c/d	10	17	5½			
				47	8	1½			

GER.

Account, No. 1.

	Cr.		L.F.	£	s.	d.	£	s.	d.
1922									
Oct. 1	By Sundry A/cs · · ·		J. 1	2721	4	3			
				2721	4	3			
	By Balance · · · ·		b/d	2514	13	7			

Account, No. 2.

	Cr.		L.F.	£	s.	d.	£	s.	d.
1923									
Feb. 28	By Cash A/c · · · ·		C.B. 2	5	0	0			
May 31	,, ,, · · · ·		,, 4	6	16	6			
June 30	,, ,, · · · ·		,, 4		11	9			
July 31	,, ,, · · · ·		,, 4	50	0	0			
	,, ,, · · · ·		,, 4	3	17	0			
Sept. 30	,, ,, · · · ·		,, 5	50	0	0			
	,, Balance · · · ·		c/d	354	9	2½			
				470	14	5½			

Account, No. 3.

	Cr.		L.F.	£	s.	d.	£	s.	d.
1922									
Oct. 31	By Cash A/c · · · ·		C.B. 1	44	6	2			
Dec. 31	,, ,, · · · ·		,, 1	15	0	10			
1923									
Sept. 30	,, Balance · · · ·		c/d	34	14	10			
				94	1	10			

Account, No. 4.

	Cr.		L.F.	£	s.	d.	£	s.	d.
1922									
Oct. 1	By Capital A/c · · · ·		J. 1	36	10	8			
1923									
Sept. 30	,, Sundry A/cs · · ·		,, 4	10	17	5½			
				47	8	1½			
	By Balance · · · ·		b/d	10	17	5½			

Horses (*Stock*)

	Dr.	L.F.	£	s.	d.	£	s.	d.
1922								
Oct. 1	*To Capital A/c*	J. 1	367	1	0			
1923								
Sept. 30	,, *Wages A/c*	,, 2	2	2	0			
	,, *Home-grown Foods A/c* .	,, 8	7	2	8			
	,, *Pastures A/c*. . . .	,, 11	20	1	4			
			396	7	0			
	To Stock on hand . . .	b/d	238	15	3			

Horses (*Working*)

		L.F.	£	s.	d.	£	s.	d.
1923								
Jan. 31	To Cash A/c	C.B. 2	1	4	0			
Apr. 30	,, ,, ...	,, 3	6	16	11			
	,, ,, ...	,, 3		5	0			
Sept. 30	,, ,, ...	,, 5	2	14	6			
	,, *Wages A/c*	J. 2	33	13	1			
	,, *Sundry Creditors A/c* .	,, 4	4	7	1			
	,, *Implements A/c* . . .	,, 6	1	13	7			
	,, *Sundry A/cs*	,, 7	139	9	6			
	Hay, oats, straw, bran, pastures and depreciation							
			190	3	8			

Cattle

		L.F.	£	s.	d.	£	s.	d.
1922								
Oct. 1	*To Capital A/c*	J. 1	481	0	0			
Nov. 30	,, Cash A/c	C.B. 1		2	0			
1923								
Mar. 31	,, ,, ...	,, 3		4	0			
Apr. 30	,, ,, ...	,, 3		4	0			
May 31	,, ,, ...	,, 4		2	0			
June 30	,, ,, ...	,, 4		2	0			
Sept. 30	,, ,, ...	,, 5		9	0			
	,, *Wages A/c*	J. 2	35	3	7			
	,, *Sundry Creditors A/c* .	,, 4	2	13	6			
	,, *Implements A/c* . . .	,, 6	1	5	11			
	,, *Horses (W) A/c* . . .	,, 7	5	14	5			
	,, *Home-grown Foods A/c* .	,, 8	80	4	9			
	,, *Straw A/c*	,, 9	18	7	5			
	,, *Sundry A/cs.* Roots . .	,, 9	24	6	9			
	,, *Establishment A/c* . .	,, 10	8	4	4			
	,, *Pastures A/c*. . . .	,, 11	124	16	2			
	,, *Cows A/c*	,, 12	67	16	6			
	,, *Cows A/c*	,, 12	15	0	0			
			865	16	4			
	To Stock on hand . . .	b/d	490	0	0			

Account, No. 5.

	Cr.	L.F.	£	s.	d.	£	s.	d.
1923								
Apr. 30	By Cash A/c	C.B. 3	54	0	9			
Sept. 30	„ *Horses (W) A/c* . .	J. 7	23	15	1			
	„ *Stock on hand* . . .	c/d	238	15	3			
	„ *Profit and Loss A/c* . .	J. 12	79	15	11			
			396	7	0			

Acccount, No. 6.

		L.F.	£	s.	d.	£	s.	d.
1923								
Sept. 30	By *Sundry A/cs* . . .	J. 5	2	14	9			
	„ *Sundry A/cs* . . .	„ 8	187	8	11			
			190	3	8			

Account, No. 7.

		L.F.	£	s.	d.	£	s.	d.
1922								
Oct. 31	By Cash A/c	C.B. 1	65	8	0			
1923								
Mar. 31	„ „	„ 3	121	19	0			
June 30	„ „	„ 4	31	2	0			
Sept. 30	„ *Stock on hand* . . .	c/d	490	0	0			
	„ *Profit and Loss A/c* . .	J. 12	157	7	4			
			865	16	4			

Cows

	Dr.	L.F.	£	s.	d.	£	s.	d.
1922								
Oct. 1	To Capital A/c	J. 1	425	0	0			
,, 31	,, Cash A/c	C.B. 1	40	6	6			
Dec. 31	,, ,, ...	,, 1		4	6			
1923								
Jan. 31	,, ,, ...	,, 2	4	4	0			
Sept. 30	,, Wages A/c . . .	J. 2	74	7	11			
	,, Implements A/c . .	,, 6	1	7	7			
	,, Horses (W) A/c . .	,, 7			11			
	,, Feeding Stuffs A/c . .	,, 8	57	19	9			
	,, Home-grown Foods A/c .	,, 8	121	10	7			
	,, Straw A/c . . .	,, 9	18	11	4			
	,, Sundry A/cs. Roots . .	,, 9	31	9	9			
	,, Establishment A/c . .	,, 10	17	3	7½			
	,, Pastures A/c . . .	,, 11	62	6	0			
	,, Profit and Loss A/c . .	,, 12	45	18	2½			
			900	10	8			
	To Stock on hand . . .	b/d	390	0	0			

Pigs

		L.F.	£	s.	d.	
1922						
Oct. 1	To Capital A/c	J. 1	60	0	0	
1923						
June 30	,, Cash A/c . . .	C.B. 4		2	6	
Sept. 30	,, Wages A/c . . .	J. 2	8	5	9	
	,, Implements A/c . .	,, 6		1	7	
	,, Horses (W) A/c . .	,, 7		5	8	
	,, Feeding Stuffs A/c .	,, 8	43	15	11	
	,, Home-grown Foods A/c .	,, 8	38	19	0	
	,, Potatoes A/c . . .	,, 9	26	15	8	
	,, Sundry A/cs. Roots . .	,, 9		12	6	
	,, Establishment A/c . .	,, 10	1	18	0	
	,, Pastures A/c . . .	,, 11	3	1	7	
			183	18	2	
	To Stock on hand . . .	b/d	62	0	0	

Account, No. 8.

	Cr.	L.F.	£	s.	d.	£	s.	d.
1922								
Oct. 31	By Cash A/c	C.B. 1	44	5	0			
Nov. 30	,, ,, ...	,, 1	31	11	9			
Dec. 31	,, ,, ...	,, 1	37	18	6			
1923								
Jan. 31	,, ,, ...	,, 2	32	7	2			
Feb. 28	,, ,, ...	,, 2	29	9	4			
Mar. 31	,, ,, ...	,, 3	23	2	4			
Apr. 30	,, ,, ...	,, 3	44	5	9			
May 31	,, ,, ...	,, 4	16	4	7			
June 30	,, ,, ...	,, 4	23	15	1			
July 31	,, ,, ...	,, 4	21	5	2			
Aug. 31	,, ,, ...	,, 5	65	12	8			
Sept. 30	,, ,, ...	,, 5	15	10	2			
	,, ,, ...	,, 5	2	15	6			
	,, *Wages A/c.* Allowance .	J. 2		17	0			
	,, *Sundry Debtors A/c* . .	,, 4	15	19	2			
	,, *Sundry A/cs.* Manurial							
	Residues . . .	,, 8	22	15	0			
	,, *Cattle A/c.* Milk to calves	,, 12	67	16	6			
	,, *Cattle A/c.* Calves . .	,, 12	15	0	0			
	,, Stock on hand . . .	c/d	390	0	0			
			900	10	8			

Account, No. 9.

		L.F.	£	s.	d.	£	s.	d.
1922								
Oct. 31	By Cash A/c	C.B. 1	33	15	6			
Nov. 30	,, ,, ...	,, 1	2	5	0			
Dec. 31	,, ,, ...	,, 1	30	7	0			
1923								
Feb. 28	,, ,, ...	,, 2	5	13	6			
June 30	,, ,, ...	,, 4	2	1	6			
	,, *Sundry A/cs.* Manurial							
	Residues . . .	J. 8	7	15	6			
	,, Stock on hand . . .	c/d	62	0	0			
	,, *Profit and Loss A/c* . .	J. 12	40	0	2			
			183	18	2			

Poultry

	Dr.	L.F.	£	s.	d.	£	s.	d.
1922 Oct. 1	To Capital A/c	J. 1	21	15	0			
1923 Sept. 30	„ Implements A/c . . .	„ 6		8	1			
	„ Home-grown Foods A/c .	„ 8	19	13	4			
			41	16	5			
	To Stock on hand . . .	b/d	21	0	0			

Hay

	Dr.	L.F.	1922 Crop			1923 Crop		
			£	s.	d.	£	s.	d.
1922 Oct. 1	To Capital A/c	J. 1	122	17	5	122	14	11
1923 Sept. 30	„ Wages A/c	„ 2				19	5	6
	„ „	„ 3		12	5	17	18	7
	„ Rent A/c	„ 4				74	6	4
	„ Implements A/c . . .	„ 6				1	12	1
	„ Horses (W) A/c . . .	„ 7				23	19	3
	„ Establishment A/c . .	„ 10				8	10	3
			123	9	10	268	6	11
			1923 Crop			1924 Crop		
	To Seed A/c . . .	J. 11				8	7	2
	„ Cost to date . . .	b/f	207	13	6			
	„ Oats 1923 A/c . . .	J. 11				15	5	5
	„ Unexhausted Costs . .	b/f				58	12	1
			207	13	6	82	4	8

Wheat

	Dr.	L.F.	1922 Crop			1923 Crop		
			£	s.	d.	£	s.	d.
1922 Oct. 1	To Capital A/c	J. 1	122	4	4	45	12	0
1923 Sept. 30	„ Wages A/c	„ 2				7	14	2
	„ „	„ 3	4	6	8	17	15	7
	„ Rent A/c	„ 4				39	16	3
	„ Horses (W) A/c . . .	„ 5		11	0			
	„ Granary A/c . . .	„ 5	15	10	0			
	„ Implements A/c . . .	„ 6				1	3	9
	„ Horses (W) A/c . . .	„ 7				27	10	5
	„ Establishment A/c . .	„ 10		19	6	5	17	4
	„ Seed	con.				13	19	0
			143	11	6	159	8	6
			1923 Crop			1924 Crop		
	To Wages A/c . . .	J. 3				1	4	5
	„ Implements A/c . . .	„ 6					1	5
	„ Horses (W) A/c . . .	„ 7				2	2	4
	„ Establishment A/c . .	„ 10					5	9
	„ Cost to date . . .	b/f	156	1	0			
	„ Beans A/c . . .	J. 11				5	12	4
			156	1	0	9	6	3

Account, No. 10.

	Cr.	L.F.	£	s.	d.	£	s.	d.
1923								
Sept. 30	By *Private A/c*	J. 12	20	16	5			
	,, Stock on hand . . .	c/d	21	0	0			
			41	16	5			

Account, No. 11.

		L.F.	1922 Crop			1923 Crop		
1923								
Sept. 30	By *Home-grown Foods A/c* .	J. 5	123	9	10			
	,, *Pastures A/c* . . .	,, 11				2	1	4
	,, Unexhausted Costs, seed,							
	sowing, manurial resi-							
	dues, etc.	c/f				58	12	1
	Cost to date . . .	,,				207	13	6
			123	9	10	268	6	11

Account, No. 12.

		L.F.	1922 Crop			1923 Crop		
1922								
Dec. 31	By Cash A/c	C.B. 1	30	16	0			
1923								
Apr. 30	,, ,, ...	,, 3	43	0	0			
July 31	,, ,, ...	,, 4	3	9	9			
Sept. 30	,, *Sundry Debtors A/c* .	J. 4	2	10	0			
	,, *Home-grown Foods A/c* .	,, 5	26	4	5			
	,, *Straw A/c*	,, 6	20	7	5			
	,, Seed	con.	13	19	0			
	,, *Peas A/c*	J. 11				3	7	6
	,, Cost to date . . .	c/f				156	1	0
	,, *Profit and Loss A/c* . .	J. 12	3	4	11			
			143	11	6	159	8	6

Barley

	Dr.	L.F.	£ s. d.	£ s. d.
1922 **Oct. 1** **1923** **Sept. 30**			*1922 Crop*	*1930 Crop*
	To Capital A/c . . .	J. 1	51 14 0	20 4 0
	,, Wages A/c	,, 2		1 13 9
	,, "	,, 3	9 9	4 5 7
	,, Rent A/c . . .	,, 4		13 5 5
	,, Granary A/c . . .	,, 5	1 11 7	
	,, Implements A/c . . .	,, 6		8 7
	,, Horses (W) A/c . .	,, 7		9 17 3
	,, Establishment A/c . .	,, 10		1 7 7
	,, Seed	con.		11 10 0
			53 15 4	62 12 2
			1923 Crop	*1924 Crop*
	To Wages A/c . . .	J. 3		19 0
	,, Implements A/c . .	,, 6		1 4
	,, Horses (W) A/c . .	,, 7		2 13 6
	,, Establishment A/c . .	,, 10		4 7
	,, Cost to date . .	b/d	62 12 2	
			62 12 2	3 18 5

Beans

			£ s. d.	£ s. d.
1922 **Oct. 1** **1923** **Sept. 30**			*1922 Crop*	*1923 Crop*
	To Capital A/c . . .	J. 1	97 11 6	
	,, Wages A/c . . .	,, 2		5 16 3
	,, " . . .	,, 3	1 3 10	17 1 9
	,, Rent A/c . . .	,, 4		18 11 7
	,, Granary A/c .	,, 5	5 10 4	
	,, Implements A/c . .	,, 6		1 4 3
	,, Horses (W) A/c . .	,, 7		23 1 5
	,, Establishment A/c .	,, 10	5 9	3 18 3
	,, Farmyard Manure A/c .	,, 10		16 17 1
	,, Seed	con.		21 2 2
			104 11 5	107 12 9
			1923 Crop	
	To Cost to date . .	b/d	102 0 5	

Account, No. 13.

	Cr.	L.F.	£	s.	d.	£	s.	d.
1923			*1922 Crop*			*1923 Crop*		
Mar. 31	By Cash A/c	C.B. 3	1	15	0			
Sept. 30	„ *Home-grown Foods A/c* .	J. 5	27	16	6			
	„ *Straw A/c*	„ 6	7	13	7			
	„ Seed	con.	11	10	0			
	„ Cost to date . . .	c/d				62	12	2
	„ *Profit and Loss A/c* . .	J. 12	5	0	3			
			53	15	4	62	12	2

Account, No. 14.

	Cr.	L.F.	£	s.	d.	£	s.	d.
1922			*1922 Crop*			*1923 Crop*		
Dec. 31	By Cash A/c	C.B. 1	32	8	0			
1923								
Sept. 30	„ „	„ 5	1	4	0			
	„ Seed	con.	21	2	2			
	„ *Wheat 1924 A/c* . .	J. 11				5	12	4
	„ Cost to date . . .	c/d				102	0	5
	„ *Profit and Loss A/c* . .	J. 12	49	17	3			
			104	11	5	107	12	9

Oats

	Dr.	L.F.	£ s. d.	£ s. d.
1922			*1922 Crop*	*1923 Crop*
Oct. 1	To Capital A/c . . .	J. 1	192 13 3	
1923				
Sept. 30	,, Wages A/c	,, 2		2 12 5
	,, ,, ...	,, 3	4 4 3	7 5 5
	,, Rent A/c	,, 4		15 18 6
	,, Horses (W) A/c . . .	,, 5	12 11	
	,, Granary A/c . . .	,, 5	10 10 2	
	,, Implements A/c . . .	,, 6		16 8
	,, Horses (W) A/c . . .	,, 8		13 2 10
	,, Sundry A/cs . . .	,, 9		28 16 7
	,, Establishment A/c . .	,, 10	19 6	2 4 10
	,, Seed	con.		10 1 0
			209 0 1	80 18 3
			1923 Crop	*1924 Crop*
	To Wages A/c . . .	J. 3		2 15 10
	,, Implements A/c . . .	,, 6		3 9
	,, Horses (W) A/c . . .	,, 8		6 5 10
	,, Establishment A/c . .	,, 10		12 8
	,, Cost to date . .	b/d	65 12 10	
			65 12 10	9 18 1

Fruit

		L.F.	£ s. d.	
1923				
July 31	To Cash A/c	C.B. 4	4 3	
Sept. 30	,, Wages A/c	J. 2	12 14 0	
	,, ,, ...	,, 3	3 0	
	,, Rent A/c	,, 4	13 5 5	
	,, Horses (W) A/c . . .	,, 7	3 3	
	,, Establishment A/c . .	,, 10	2 18 8	
	,, Profit and Loss A/c . .	,, 12	14 6 1	
			43 14 8	

Peas

		L.F.	£ s. d.	£ s. d.
1923			*1923 Crop*	*1924 Crop*
Sept. 30	To Wages A/c	J. 2	52 13 11	
	,, ,, ...	,, 3	18 15 7	
	,, Rent A/c	,, 4	15 18 6	
	,, Implements A/c . . .	,, 6	1 6 5	
	,, Horses (W) A/c . . .	,, 7	28 5 11	
	,, Establishment A/c . .	,, 10	14 0 9	
	,, Farmyard Manure A/c .	,, 10	14 9 4	
	,, Seed A/c	,, 11	48 8 3	
	,, Wheat 1923 A/c . . .	,, 11		3 7 6
			193 18 8	3 7 6
				1924 Crop
	To Cost to date . . .	b/d		3 7 6

Account, No. 15.

	Cr.	L.F.	£ s. d.	£ s. d.
1923			*1922 Crop*	*1923 Crop*
Jan. 31	By Cash A/c	C.B. 2	3 4 0	
Sept. 30	,, *Home-grown Foods A/c* .	J. 5	161 11 8	
	,, *Straw A/c*	,, 6	29 14 4	
	,, Seed	con.	10 1 0	
	,, *Hay A/c*	J. 11		15 5 5
	,, Cost to date . . .	c/d		65 12 10
	,, *Profit and Loss A/c* . .	J. 12	4 9 1	
			209 0 1	80 18 3

Account, No. 16.

1922				
Nov. 30	By Cash A/c	C.B. 1	3 12 0	
Dec. 31	,, ,, ...	,, 1	1 16 0	
1923				
Apr. 30	,, ,, ...	,, 3	2 0 0	
Aug. 31	,, ,, ...	,, 5	33 6 0	
Sept. 30	,, *Sundry Debtors A/c* . .	J. 4	3 0 8	
			43 14 8	

Account, No. 17.

1922			*1923 Crop*	*1924 Crop*
Dec. 31	By Cash A/c	C.B. 1	1 15 0	
1923				
July 31	,, ,, ...	,, 4	9 9 0	
Aug. 31	,, ,, ...	,, 5	35 0 0	
Sept. 30	,, ,, ...	,, 5	141 1 0	
	,, Cost to date . . .	c/d		3 7 6
	,, *Profit and Loss A/c* . .	J. 12	6 13 8	
			193 18 8	3 7 6

Swedes and

	Dr.	L.F.	£ s. d.	£ s. d.
			1922 Crop	*1923 Crop*
1922 Oct. 1	To Capital A/c	J. 1	51 11 8	
1923 Sept. 30	,, Wages A/c	,, 3	4 5 4	
	,, Rent A/c	,, 4		3 19 8
	,, Implements A/c . . .	,, 6		4 2
	,, Horses (W) A/c . . .	,, 7	2 10	
	,, Potatoes A/c	,, 9		1 15 1
	,, Mangolds A/c . . .	,, 11		7 8 0
			55 19 10	13 6 11
			1923 Crop	
	To Cost to date . . .	b/d	13 6 11	

Mangolds

			£ s. d.	£ s. d.
			1922 Crop	*1923 Crop*
1922 Oct. 1	To Capital A/c	J. 1	50 6 9	
1923 Sept. 30	,, Wages A/c	,, 2		6 13 6
	,, ,,	,, 3	13 13 0	9 13 5
	,, Rent A/c	,, 4		3 19 7
	,, Implements A/c . . .	,, 6		4 2
	,, Horses (W) A/c . . .	,, 7	11 2 8	11 6 5
	,, Potatoes A/c	,, 9		1 15 1
	,, Seed A/c	,, 11		18 6
			75 2 5	34 10 8
			1923 Crop	
	To Cost to date . . .	o/d	27 2 8	

Potatoes

			£ s. d.	£ s. d.
			1922 Crop	*1923 Crop*
1922 Oct. 1	To Capital A/c	J. 1	45 17 4	38 9 4
1923 Sept. 30	,, Wages A/c	,, 2	3 4 3	
	,, ,,	,, 3	14 16 3	5 6 2
	,, Rent A/c	,, 4		2 13 1
	,, Implements A/c . . .	,, 6		18 9
	,, Horses (W) A/c . . .	,, 7	18 10	8 3 11
	,, Seed	con.		6 12 3
			64 16 8	62 3 6
			1923 Crop	
	To Cost to date . . .	b/d	62 3 6	

Turnips Account, No. 18.

	Cr.	L.F.	£ s. d.	£ s. d.
1923			*1922 Crop*	*1923 Crop*
Sept. 30	By *Sundry Debtors A/c* . .	J. 4	12 0 0	
	„ *Oats A/c*	„ 9	15 0 2	
	„ *Sundry A/cs* . . .	„ 9	23 18 2	
	„ *Cost to date* . . .	c/d		13 6 11
	„ *Profit and Loss A/c* . .	J. 12	5 1 6	
			55 19 10	13 6 11

Account, No. 19.

		L.F.	£ s. d.	£ s. d.
1923			*1922 Crop*	*1923 Crop*
June 30	By Cash A/c	C.B. 4	7 14 0	
July 31	„ „	„ 4	5 2 6	
Aug. 31	„ „	„ 5	1 10 0	
Sept. 30	„ *Sundry Debtors A/c* .	J. 4	1 5 0	
	„ *Oats A/c*	„ 9	13 16 5	
	„ *Sundry A/cs* . . .	„ 9	32 10 10	
	„ *Swedes A/c* . . .	„ 11		7 8 0
	„ *Cost to date* . . .	c/d		27 2 8
	„ *Profit and Loss A/c* .	J 12	13 3 8	
			75 2 5	34 10 8

Account, No. 20.

		L.F.	£ s. d.	£ s. d.
1922			*1922 Crop*	*1923 Crop*
Oct. 31	By Cash A/c	C.B. 1	1 0 0	
1923				
June 30	„ „	„ 4	4 0 3	
July 31	„ „	„ 4	1 0 0	
Sept. 30	„ *Sundry A/cs* . . .	J. 9	3 10 2	
	„ *Pigs A/c*	„ 9	26 15 8	
	„ *Seed*	con.	6 12 3	
	„ *Cost to date* . . .	c/d		62 3 6
	„ *Profit and Loss A/c* . .	J. 12	21 18 4	
			64 16 8	62 3 6

Pastures

	Dr.	L.F.	£	s.	d.	£	s.	d.
1922								
Oct. 1	To *Capital A/c*	J. 1	48	8	5			
1923								
Sept. 30	,, *Wages A/c*	,, 3	5	15	1			
	,, *Rent A/c*	,, 4	209	16	3			
	,, *Implements A/c* . . .	,, 6		8	1			
	,, *Horses (W) A/c* . . .	,, 8		8	6			
	,, *Sundry A/cs.* Manurial							
	Residues	,, 8	10	1	0			
	,, *Hay A/c*	,, 11	2	1	4			
			276	18	8			
	To Unexhausted Costs . .	b/d	34	9	0			

Granary

		L.F.	£	s.	d.	£	s.	d.
1923			*1922*			*1923*		
Mar. 31	To Cash A/c	C.B. 3		16	8			
Apr. 30	,, ,, ...	,, 3		16	8			
May 31	,, ,, ...	,, 4	12	7	6			
Sept. 30	,, ,, ...	,, 5	12	7	6			
	,, *Wages A/c*	J. 2	3	15	0			
	,, ,, ...	,, 2	1	14	11			
	,, *Horses (W) A/c* . . .	,, 5	1	3	10	1	0	0
	,, ,, ,, . . .	,, 7					18	4
	,, *Straw A/c*	,, 9				3	0	8
			33	2	1	4	19	0
			1923					
	To Costs to date . . .	b/d	4	19	0			

Implements

		L.F.	£	s.	d.	£	s.	d.
1922								
Oct. 1	To *Capital A/c*	J. 1	229	11	6			
Dec. 31	,, Cash A/c	C.B. 1		2	9			
1923								
Sept. 30	,, ,, ...	,, 5	6	0	0			
	,, *Wages A/c*	J. 2	1	12	9			
	,, *Horses (W) A/c* . . .	,, 5		7	0			
			237	14	0			
	To Stock on hand . . .	b/d	212	12	6			

Account, No. 21.

	Cr.	L.F.	£	s.	d.	£	s.	d.
1923 Sept. 30	By *Horses* (*W*) *A/c* . . .	J. 7	32	4	7			
	„ Unexhausted Costs and							
	residues of manure .	c/d	34	9	0			
	„ *Sundry A/cs* . . .	J. 11	210	5	1			
			276	18	8			

Account, No. 22.

	Cr.	L.F.	*1922*			*1923*		
1923 Sept. 30	By *Sundry A/cs* . . .	J. 5	33	2	1			
	„ *Costs* (1923) to date . .	c/d				4	19	0
			33	2	1	4	19	0

Account, No. 23.

	Cr.	L.F.	£	s.	d.
1923 Sept. 30	By *Sundry A/cs* . . .	J. 6	25	1	6
	„ Stock on hand . . .	c/d	212	12	6
			237	14	0

Tools and Small

	Dr.	L.F.	£	s.	d.	£	s.	d.
1922								
Oct. 1	To Capital A/c	J. 1	5	11	10			
1923								
Apr. 30	,, Cash A/c	C.B. 3		5	4			
Aug. 31	,, ,, ...	,, 5	1	0	0			
			6	17	2			
	To Stock on hand . . .	b/d	5	9	6			

Feeding Stuffs

		L.F.	£	s.	d.	£	s.	d.
1922								
Oct. 1	To Capital A/c	J. 1	42	1	10			
Dec. 31	,, Cash A/c	C.B. 1	15	19	0			
1923								
Feb. 28	,, ,, ...	,, 2	28	16	11			
Mar. 31	,, ,, ...	,, 3	9	18	9			
Sept. 30	,, ,, ...	,, 5	23	9	1			
	,, Wages A/c	J. 2		12	3			
	,, Horses (W) A/c . . .	,, 7	1	5	5			
			122	3	3			
	To Stock on hand . . .	b/d	11	11	2			

Insurance

		L.F.	£	s.	d.	£	s.	d.
1922								
Oct. 1	To Capital A/c	J. 1	6	19	2			
	To Establishment A/c . .	,, 10	7	5	7			
	Premium in advance							

Seed

		L.F.	£	s.	d.	£	s.	d.
1922								
Dec. 31	To Cash A/c	C.B. 1	7	11	0			
1923								
Mar. 31	,, ,, ...	,, 3	40	15	9			
Apr. 30	,, ,, ...	,, 3	9	5	8			
Sept. 30	,, Wages A/c	J. 2			7			
	,, Horses (W) A/c . . .	,, 7			11			
			57	13	11			

Implements Account, No. 24.

	Cr.	L.F.	£	s.	d.	£	s.	d.
1923 Sept. 30	By *Establishment A/c* . .	J. 6	1	7	8			
	,, Stock on hand . . .	c/d	5	9	6			
			6	17	2			

Account, No. 25.

			£	s.	d.
1923 Sept. 30	By *Home-grown Foods A/c*	J. 5	4	11	5
	,, *Horses (W) A/c* . . .	,, 7	4	5	0
	,, *Sundry A/cs* . . .	,, 8	101	15	8
	Foods consumed				
	,, Stock on hand . . .	c/d	11	11	2
			122	3	3

Account, No. 26.

			£	s.	d.
1923 Sept. 30	By *Establishment A/c* . .	J. 10	6	19	2

Account, No. 27.

			£	s.	d.
1923 Sept. 30	By *Sundry A/cs* . . .	J. 11	57	13	11
			57	13	11

Rent, Rates and

	Dr.	L.F.	£	s.	d.	£	s.	d.
1923								
Jan. 31	To Cash A/c	C.B. 2	170	0	0			
Feb. 28	,, ,, ...	,, 2	37	0	1			
Apr. 30	,, ,, ...	,, 3	8	6	0			
July 31	,, ,, ...	,, 4	209	0	6			
Sept. 30	,, ,, ...	,, 5	2	16	0			
	,, Rent owing	c/f	170	0	0			
			597	2	7			

Establishment

		L.F.	£	s.	d.
1922					
Oct. 31	To Cash A/c	C.B. 1		3	4
Nov. 30	,, ,, ...	,, 1		3	2
Dec. 31	,, ,, ...	,, 1		3	3½
1923					
Jan. 31	,, ,, ...	,, 2	3	14	8
	,, ,, ...	,, 2	1	4	10
Feb. 28	,, ,, ...	,, 2	2	5	0
	,, ,, ...	,, 2		6	10½
Mar. 31	,, ,, ...	,, 3	3	2	2
Apr. 30	,, ,, ...	,, 3		10	3
May 31	,, ,, ...	,, 4		4	5
June 30	,, ,, ...	,, 4		1	9
July 31	,, ,, ...	,, 4		14	2
Aug. 31	,, ,, ...	,, 5	1	12	10
Sept. 30	,, ,, ...	,, 5	9	2	7
	,, ,, ...	,, 5		2	3
	,, *Wages A/c*	J. 2	15	5	0
	,, *Sundry Creditors A/c* .	,, 4	3	16	10½
	,, *Implements A/c* . . .	,, 6	11	11	4
	,, *Tools A/c*	,, 6	1	7	8
	,, *Horses (W) A/c* . . .	,, 7	2	16	10
	,, *Sundry A/cs* . . .	,, 10	18	7	8
			76	16	11½

Sundries

		L.F.	£	s.	d.
1922					
Dec. 31	To Cash A/c	C.B. 1	1	10	0
1923					
Sept. 30	,, *Profit and Loss A/c* . .	J. 12	1	0	0
			2	10	0

Taxes Account, No. 28.

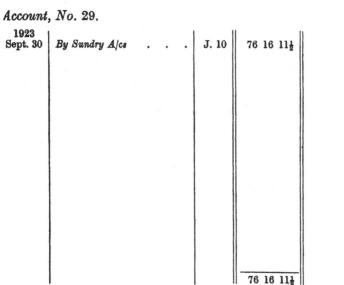

	Cr.	L.F.	£	s.	d.	£	s.	d.
1922 Oct. 1	By Capital A/c	J. 1	170	0	0			
1923 Sept. 30	,, Wages A/c. Allowances to men	,, 2	15	12	0			
	,, Sundry A/cs . . .	,, 4	411	10	7			
	Apportionment at 53s. 1d. per acre							
			597	2	7			
	By Rent owing . . .	b/f	170	0	0			

Account, No. 29.

1923 Sept. 30	By Sundry A/cs . . .	J. 10	76	16	11½			
			76	16	11½			

Account, No. 30.

1923 Feb. 28	By Cash A/c	C.B. 2	2	10	0			
			2	10	0			

o

Wages

	Dr.	L.F.	£	s.	d.	£	s.	d.
1922								
Oct. 1	To *Capital A/c*	J. 1		12	6			
,, 31	,, Cash A/c	C.B. 1	31	6	0			
Nov. 30	,, ,, ...	,, 1	42	5	0			
Dec. 31	,, ,, ...	,, 1	34	10	0			
1923								
Jan. 31	,, ,, ...	,, 2	25	0	0			
Feb. 28	,, ,, ...	,, 2	20	15	0			
Mar. 31	,, ,, ...	,, 3	32	1	0			
Apr. 30	,, ,, ...	,, 3	22	8	0			
May 31	,, ,, ...	,, 4	34	13	0			
June 30	,, ,, ...	,, 4	26	11	6			
July 31	,, ,, ...	,, 4	19	4	10			
	,, ,, ...	,, 4	45	17	6			
Aug. 31	,, ,, ...	,, 5	39	15	8			
	,, ,, ...	,, 5	17	18	0			
Sept. 30	,, ,, ...	,, 5	46	12	0			
	,, *Sundry A/cs.* Allowances	J. 2	16	9	0			
			455	19	0			
	To Insurance Stamps on hand	b/d	1	0	0			

Fences

		L.F.	£	s.	d.	£	s.	d.
1923								
Mar. 31	To Cash A/c	C.B. 3	1	0	4			
Sept. 30	,, *Wages A/c* . . .	J. 2	9	18	9			
	,, *Horses (W) A/c* . . .	,, 7		9	5			
			11	8	6			

Farmyard Manure

		L.F.	£	s.	d.	£	s.	d.
1922								
Oct. 1	To *Capital A/c*	J. 1	10	10	1			
1923								
Sept. 30	,, *Wages A/c*	,, 2	2	1	2			
	,, *Horses (W) A/c* . . .	,, 7	5	13	0			
	,, *Sundry A/cs.* Manurial							
	Residues	,, 8	20	9	6			
	,, *Straw A/c*	,, 9	15	16	3			
			54	10	0			
	To Stock on hand . .	b/d	23	3	7			

Account, No. 31.

		L.F.	£	s.	d.	£	s.	d.
	Dr.							
1923 Sept. 30	By *Sundry A/cs* . . . Special rates, piece-work, etc.	J. 2	116	2	9			
	„ *Sundry A/cs* . . . Flat rate apportioned	„ 3	338	16	3			
	„ Insurance Stamps on hand	c/d	1	0	0			
			455	19	0			

Account, No. 32.

		L.F.	£	s.	d.
1923 Sept. 30	By *Establishment A/c* . .	J. 10	11	8	6
			11	8	6

Account, No. 33.

		L.F.	£	s.	d.
1923 Sept. 30	By *Sundry A/cs* . . .	J. 10	31	6	5
	„ Stock on hand . . .	c/d	23	3	7
			54	10	0

Home-grown Foods

		L.F.	£	s.	d.	£	s.	d.
	Dr.							
1923								
Sept. 30	*To Sundry A/cs* . . .	J. 5	339	2	5			
	Hay, wheat, oats, barley							
	,, *Feeding Stuffs A/c* . .	,, 5	4	11	5			
			343	13	10			

Straw

		L.F.	£	s.	d.	£	s.	d.
1922								
Sept. 30	*To Wages A/c*	J. 3		7	7			
	,, *Sundry A/cs* . . .	,, 6	57	15	4			
	,, *Horses (W) A/c* . . .	,, 7		18	10			
			59	1	9			
	To Stock on hand . . .	b/d		4	9			

Profit and Loss

		L.F.	£	s.	d.	£	s.	d.
1923								
Sept. 30	*To Sundry A/cs:*	J. 12						
	Horses (S)	L.F. 5	79	15	11			
	Cattle	,, 7	157	7	4			
	Pigs	,, 9	40	0	2			
	Wheat	,, 12	3	4	11			
	Barley	,, 13	5	0	3			
	Beans	,, 14	49	17	3			
	Oats	,, 15	4	9	1			
	Peas	,, 17	6	13	8			
	Swedes and turnips . .	,, 18	5	1	6			
	Mangolds	,, 19	13	3	8			
	Potatoes	,, 20	21	18	4			
			386	12	1			

Balance Sheet as at

	£	s.	d.	£	s.	d.
Dr.						
Liabilities						
Rent owing	170	0	0			
Sundry Creditors . .	10	17	5½			
Cash at bank overdrawn .	1	11	3			
Capital A/c	2514	13	7			
	2697	2	3½			

Account, No. 34.

	Cr.	L.F.	£	s.	d.	£	s.	d.
1923 Sept. 30	By *Horses* (*W*) *A/c* . . .	J. 7	76	3	6			
	„ *Sundry Stock A/cs* . .	„ 8	267	10	4			
	Hay, wheat, oats and barley consumed							
			343	13	10			

Account, No. 35.

	Cr.	L.F.	£	s.	d.	£	s.	d.
1923 Sept. 30	By *Horses* (*W*) *A/c* . . .	J. 7	3	1	4			
	„ *Sundry A/cs* . . .	„ 9	55	15	8			
	„ Stock on hand . . .	c/d		4	9			
			59	1	9			

Account, No. 36.

	Cr.	L.F.	£	s.	d.	£	s.	d.
1923 Sept. 30	By *Sundry A/cs* . . .	J. 12						
	Cows	L.F. 8	45	18	2½			
	Fruit	„ 16	14	6	1			
	Sundries	„ 30	1	0	0			
	Private A/c, being loss on year's farming . .	J. 13	325	7	9½			
			386	12	1			

September 30, 1923.

Cr.	£	s.	d.	£	s.	d.
Assets						
Private A/c	354	9	2½			
Sundry Debtors . . .	34	14	10			
Live-stock	1201	15	3			
Crops and Cultivations . .	845	0	8			
Implements and Tools . .	218	2	0			
Stores	34	14	9			
Insurance paid in advance .	7	5	7			
National Health Insurance Stamps	1	0	0			
	2697	2	3½			

CHAPTER VII

CONCLUSIONS AND DEDUCTIONS

IT is now possible to consider what information is furnished by the completed accounts, but in drawing conclusions it must be remembered that these are the results of one year's farming only, and the circumstances attending the year's work must always be borne in mind. As time goes by, costs and other data will accumulate, and each succeeding year will give additional reliability to the figures; it is this accumulation of evidence that acts as a guide to the development and control of the enterprise.

Taking the accounts as they come in the Ledger, the *Capital Account* (p. 110) shows the net amount of the farmer's investment in his farm, namely £2514. 13s. 7d. The *Private Account* (p. 110) shows the personal transactions which the farmer has had on the farm bank account. It is charged with certain sums drawn by him from time to time, and credited, on the other hand, with payments into the bank. It is charged, also, with the value of the poultry consumed in the farm-house, and with the amount of the year's farming loss. The net result is that the account shows the farmer as owing £354. 9s. 2½d. to the farm account.

The *Sundry Debtors Account* (p. 110) tells that there are debts due to the farm amounting in all to £34. 14s. 10d. The details are got by reference to the Journal, folio 4.

Similarly, the *Sundry Creditors Account* (p. 110) indicates the debts owing by the farm.

The *Horses (Stock) Account* (p. 112) indicates that the transactions in horses have resulted in a loss of £79. 15s. 11d.

The *Horses (Working) Account* (p. 112) is important. It gives the cost of keeping the work horses on the farm, namely £190. 3s. 8d. From the number of horses the cost per horse can be ascertained; and from the number of hours worked, the cost per hour appears. In this case it amounted to 11·3d. per hour. By comparison of this figure year by year, the manager is led to detect any inefficiency in the organisation of the horse-labour on the farm.

The *Cows Account* (p. 114) shows the profit made and allows the cost of keeping the herd to be ascertained; a comparison of this cost, with the number of gallons of milk recorded gives the farmer the cost per gallon. Further, by summarising the various components of the total cost, he can analyse the gallon cost; he can see, year by year, how his expenditure on labour, foods, etc., per gallon, fluctuates, and by the comparison of his figures with those of others his attention is directed to possible economies.

The *Pig Account* and the *Poultry Account* do not present any new features. Passing on to the crop accounts, the first is that for *Hay* (p. 116). The farmer very commonly has the hay from two years' crops on hand at the same time, and in the place of opening separate accounts for each the Ledger is provided with double money columns, one for each year, and the entries posted to the account are carried to their appropriate column. At the close of the year the columns are, of course, balanced independently. In this case the columns for the 1922 hay crop show the cost of hay on hand at the beginning of the year, a small additional labour cost, and the transfer of the whole to the Home-grown Foods Account, on p. 132. The debit column of the 1923 crop shows the gross costs incurred in its production up to the close of the financial year, and when credit has been taken for the grazing of the after-math, and for the manures still unexhausted in the land, the net cost of the 1923 crop remains. By making an estimate of the weight of hay, the cost per ton can be deduced.

The accounts for the *Grain Crops* which follow are of a similar character, and can be used to furnish similar information.

The *Fruit Account* (p. 120) gives the cost of this crop, and the profit made; and the three *Root Crop* accounts present no new features.

Pastures Account (p. 124) shows the cost of the year's grazing. The Farmyard Manure Account (p. 130), enables the cost per load of manure to be ascertained, and not infrequently leads the farmer to consider economies in feeding by reason of the high cost of cake-fed dung.

The rest of the accounts call for no particular mention, and there remains only the Profit and Loss Account and the Balance Sheet. The *Profit and Loss Account* (p. 132) consists of *net* profit or loss balances from the various departments of the business, and its balance is the net profit or loss (in this case a loss) on the year's working of the whole.

A study of the *Balance Sheet* (p. 132) makes it at once apparent that this provides a complete statement of the financial position of the business. The liabilities indicate the amount of money invested in the business, and the sources from which it comes. In this case some of it has been provided by the farmer; some is borrowed, so to speak, from the persons to whom there are debts due—the landlord and the sundry creditors; some again, a small amount in this case, is borrowed from the bank on overdraft. The total liability, £2697. 2s. 3½d., must be balanced by realisable assets if the ostensible position is justifiable, so that a careful scrutiny of the assets is always called for when considering any balance sheet. The case presented here furnishes a good example. The items for Insurance Stamps in hand and Insurance premium paid in advance are clearly "good"; continuing up the list, the next four items represent the valuations of the live and dead stock on the farm, and as these have been made on the basis of cost, or of cost less depreciation in certain cases, the figures may be taken as fairly conservative. The next item is that for sundry debtors; the amount involved is small, and there is no reason to suppose that the sums due to the farm will not be paid, so that this asset, too, may be regarded as good. Lastly, there is the sum of £354. 9s. 2½d. due by the farmer to the farm. This is the weak element in the balance sheet; it consists mainly of the loss of £325. 7s. 9½d. on the year's working, and the soundness of the balance sheet depends upon the capacity of the farm to make the loss good in future years, or on the ability of the farmer to refund the money from other resources.

In studying a balance sheet, then, the points to con-sider are, first, the valuation of the working plant and stocks of goods on hand; second, the financial stability of the sundry debtors; third, when the balance of the profit and loss account has to be included amongst the assets, either directly, or hidden in the balance of the Private Account, the prospects of its being wiped out by better trade in the future. Unless these points can be satisfactorily met the assets cannot be regarded as a set-off to the liabilities, and the capital shown as invested in the farm is more than could be realised if the enterprise had to be wound up.

In conclusion it should be stated that no finality is claimed for the forms and processes recommended in this volume; they are mainly adduced for the purpose of aiding the farmer and the student in the study of the principles of costing as applied to the agricultural industry. These principles are easily mastered, and their application entails no profound knowledge of accountancy, but the problems which arise vary with varying styles of farming. Nothing is more to be desired, therefore, than that the individual, keeping clear in his mind the idea of working to ascertain the cost of production, should devise the means to that end specially suited to his own case, and that he should not allow himself to be bound by any rigid system. It must be remembered, too, that these accounts are essentially *management* accounts, designed only to enable the farmer to control the development of his enterprise. They are not intended, primarily, for purposes of audit, and where it is necessary to present books for annual examination and certification by an auditor cost accounts such as these would be linked up with a system of ordinary financial accounts, which alone need be submitted for audit.

INDEX

Printed in the United States
By Bookmasters